Kitty LiBBer

Kitty Libber

Cat Cartoons by Women

Edited by Rosalind Warren

The Crossing Press, Freedom, California 95019

Many of the designs in *Kitty Libber* are available from the individual artists in the form of postcards, t-shirts, coffee mugs, etc. For more information contact Rosalind Warren at P.O. Box 259, Bala Cynwyd, PA 19004.

The Funny Times (3108 Scarborough Road, Cleveland Heights, Ohio 44118) and *Comic Relief Magazine* (P.O. Box 6606, Eureka, CA 95502) feature the work of several of the cartoonists in *Kitty Libber*. And watch for Nichole Hollander's forthcoming cat humor book—*Everything Here is Mine: Sylvia's Unhelpful Guide to Cat Behavior*.

Cover cartoon by Diane Dimassa

Cover design by AnneMarie Arnold

Interior design by Amy Sibiga

Printed in the U.S.A.

Library of Congress Cataloging in Publication Data

Kitty libber: cat cartoons by women/edited by Rosalind Warren.

p. cm.

ISBN 0-89594-539-8

1. Cats—Caricatures and cartoons. 2. Wit and humor, Pictorial.

I. Warren, Rosalind, 1954-

NC1763.C35K58 1992

741.5—dc20 91-45114

CIP

Dedication

Kitty Libber is respectfully dedicated to my cat Louisa and to the cats who inspired the cartoonists whose work appears in this book:

Julia, Tao, Tamino, Stinky, Peanut, Binky, Puff, Tiger, Satin, Daisy, Kotik, Emma, Joey, Sidney (The Grump), Miz Willoughby, Jitterbug, Alexandra Nightie-case, Pru Pru Grunties, Zabu, The Sabre-gummed Tiger, Percival the Bold (also known as Fluffy Balls), Queen Lupin (also known as Bloody Animal). Diana, Sashia, Munchkin, Riri, Goalie Jane Wilson, Frank, Iggy, Poppy-noid, Fluffy Eastwood, Mr. Bean, Widget, The Little Prince, Tootie, Zachary, Herbert, Christmas, Wova, Bosco, Spooky, Tiny, Muffy, Cokie, Emily, Cupcake, Sunshine, Johnny, Pew, Cat-Face, Moggins, Rosemary, Baron, Geofurry, Bundle, Dorren, Florence Bightingale, Hobie, Rug, Prudence Louise, Wotan, Moglet, Mogadon, Boris, Daisy, Big Boy, Isaac, Mickey, Emil, Poguie, Redford, Eddie, Willa, Barney, Wilma, Tippy, Sweety, Fiona, Shanti, Spaide (the cat who thinks he's a dog), Strother, Starember, Reynard, Rufus, Marlo, Motsie, A Cat Named Hercules, Snowy, Ms. Wuff, Osiris, Beancake, Pipi, Rupert, Fred, Roosevelt, Audrey, Tootsie, Patton, Godzilla, Sheba, Whiskers, Porky, Nadger, Marcel, Jake Quinn, Buzz Majoun, Jumbo, Vorrie, Basil, Poppy, Emily, Kirnen, Miss Kitty and, of course, Pierre.

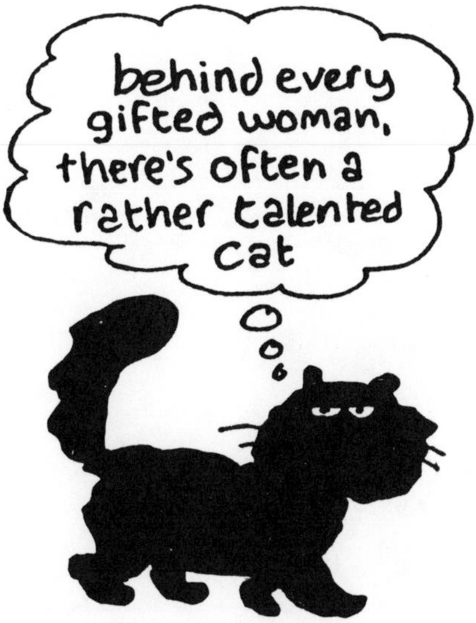
behind every gifted woman, there's often a rather talented cat

Viv Quillin

The Contributors
(in alphabetical order)

Alison Bechdel

Judy Becker

Suzy Becker

Anne Beidler

Jennifer Berman

Lee Binswanger

Claire Bretecher

Dean Brittingham

Martha Campbell

Jennifer Camper

Roz Chast

Denny Derbyshire

Rhonda Dicksion

Diane Dimassa

Wendy Eastwood

Sharone Einhorn

Leslie Ewing

Karen Favreau

Kate Gawf

Anne Gibbons

Nikki Gosch

Roberta Gregory

Terry Harned

Elizabeth Hay

Marian Henley

Joan Hilty

Housewives in Hell

Cath Jackson

Lee Kennedy

Kris Kovick

Annie Lawson

Mary Lawton

Kathryn Lemieux

Theresa McCracken

Cinders McLeod

Alice Muhlback

Andrea Natalie

Nina Paley

Rina Piccolo

Stephanie Piro

Viv Quillin

Dianne Reum

Trina Robbins

Christine Roche

Ursula Roma

Flash Rosenberg

Posy Simmonds

Chris Suddick

Mette Thomsen

Carole Tyrrell

Julia Willis

Penny Yrigoyen

Roberta Gregory

Well. I'm HOME... I WORKED all day, and YOU'RE in the exact same spot where I left you this morning...
The next sound I hear had better be the CAN OPENER..

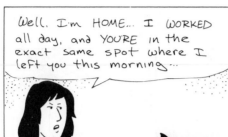

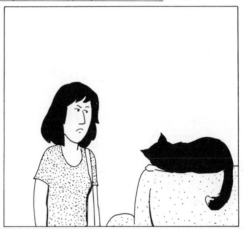

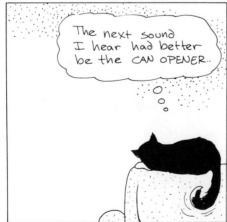

Marian Henley

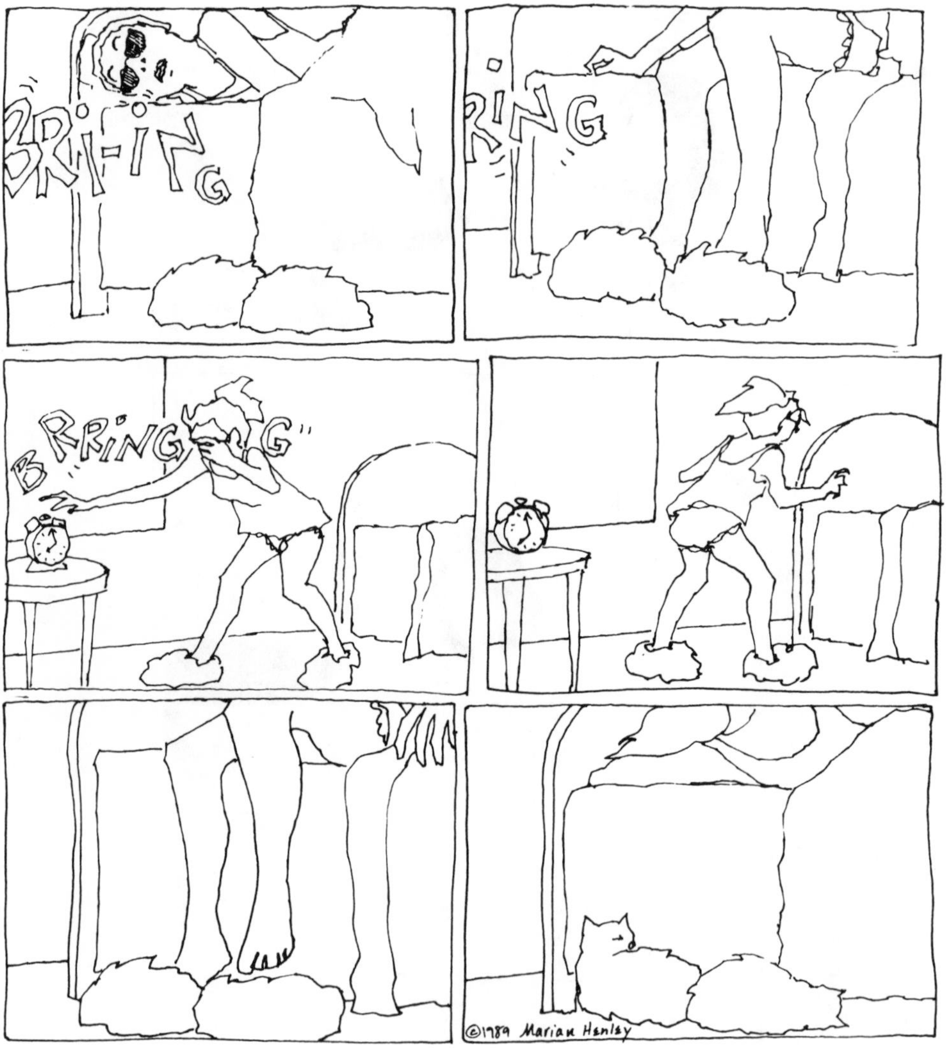

BRI-ING
RING
BRRING G
©1989 Marian Henley

CAT FADS

OF APARTMENT 11-N

For a while, anything "in creamy gravy" was the thing. Then suddenly, nothing but tuna would do.

The blue chair was big last month, but this month, it's the far right corner of the livingroom.

Finally, one wonders why the beloved dented ping pong ball of a week ago is now just so much dross

R. Chast

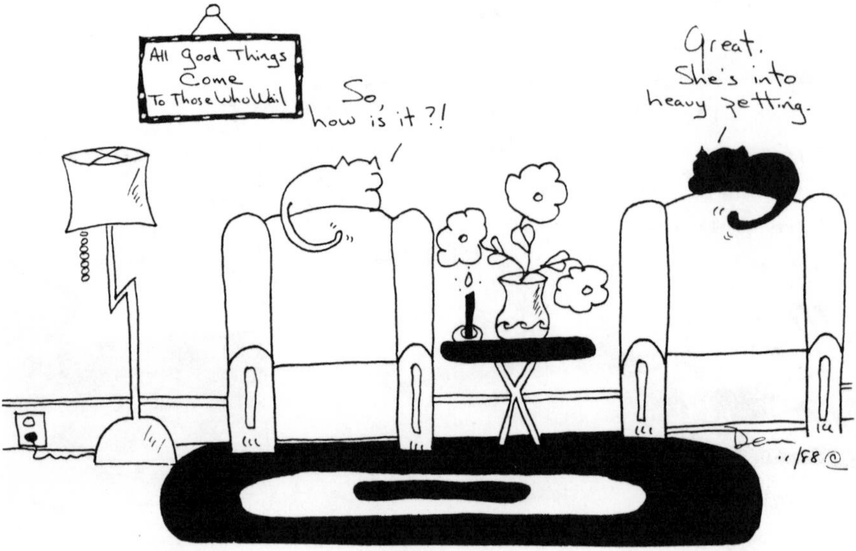
All Good Things
Come
To Those Who Wait
So, how is it ?!
Great. She's into heavy petting.
Dean '88 ©

Nina Paley

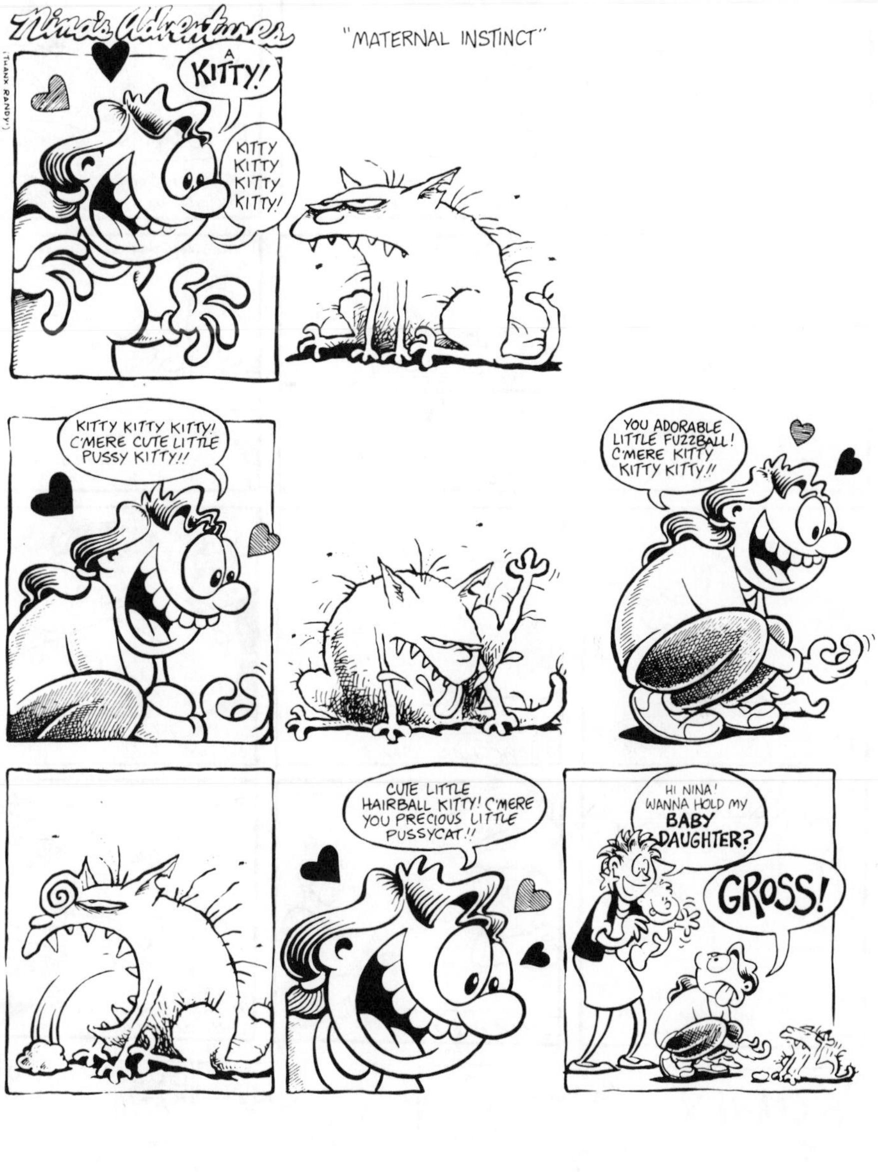
Nina's Adventures
"MATERNAL INSTINCT"
(THANX RANDY!)
A KITTY!
KITTY KITTY KITTY KITTY!
KITTY KITTY KITTY! C'MERE CUTE LITTLE PUSSY KITTY!!
YOU ADORABLE LITTLE FUZZBALL! C'MERE KITTY KITTY KITTY!!
CUTE LITTLE HAIRBALL KITTY! C'MERE YOU PRECIOUS LITTLE PUSSYCAT!!
HI NINA! WANNA HOLD MY BABY DAUGHTER?
GROSS!

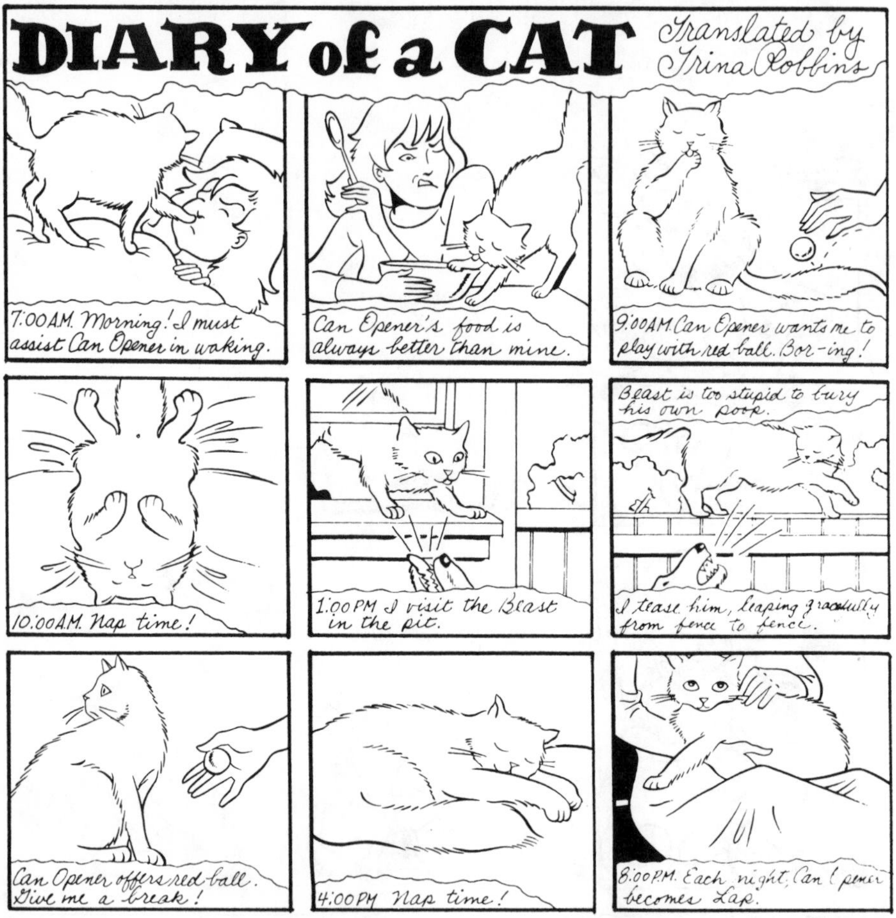
DIARY of a CAT
Translated by Trina Robbins
7:00 A.M. Morning! I must assist Can Opener in waking.
Can Opener's food is always better than mine.
9:00 A.M. Can Opener wants me to play with red ball. Bor-ing!
10:00 A.M. Nap time!
1:00 PM I visit the Beast in the pit.
Beast is too stupid to bury his own poop.
I tease him, leaping gracefully from fence to fence.
Can Opener offers red ball. Give me a break!
4:00 PM Nap time!
8:00 P.M. Each night, Can Opener becomes Lap.
9:00 P.M. All admire my beauty and cleverness.
10:00 P.M. Nap time!
4:00 A.M. Time to play with red ball.

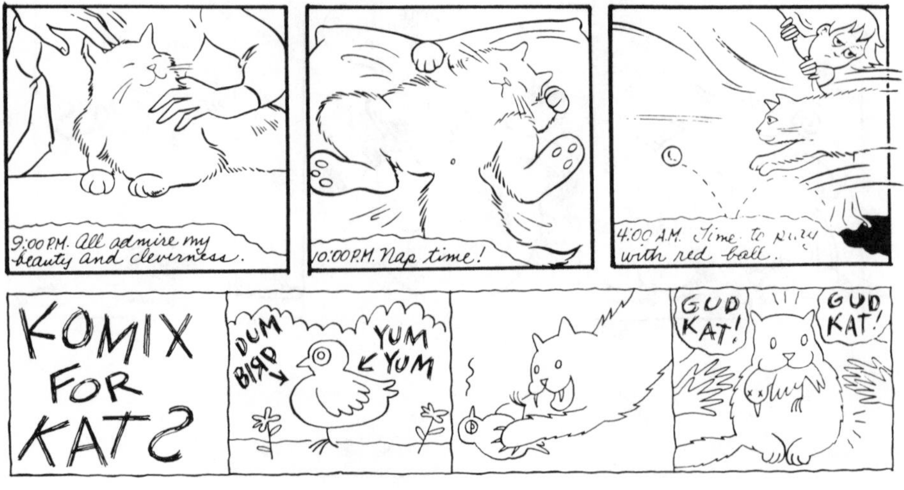
KOMIX FOR KATS
DUM BIRD
YUM YUM
GUD KAT!
GUD KAT!

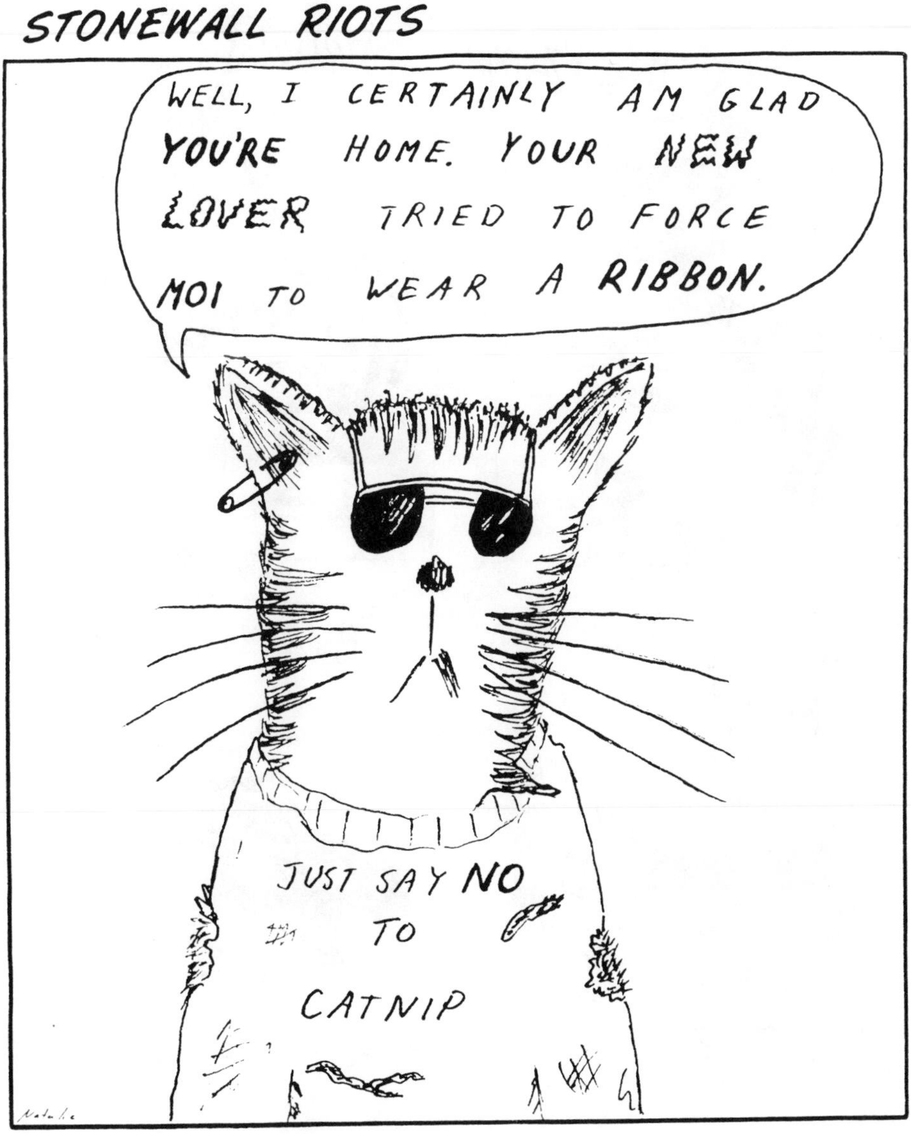
STONEWALL RIOTS
WELL, I CERTAINLY AM GLAD YOU'RE HOME. YOUR NEW LOVER TRIED TO FORCE MOI TO WEAR A RIBBON.
JUST SAY NO TO CATNIP

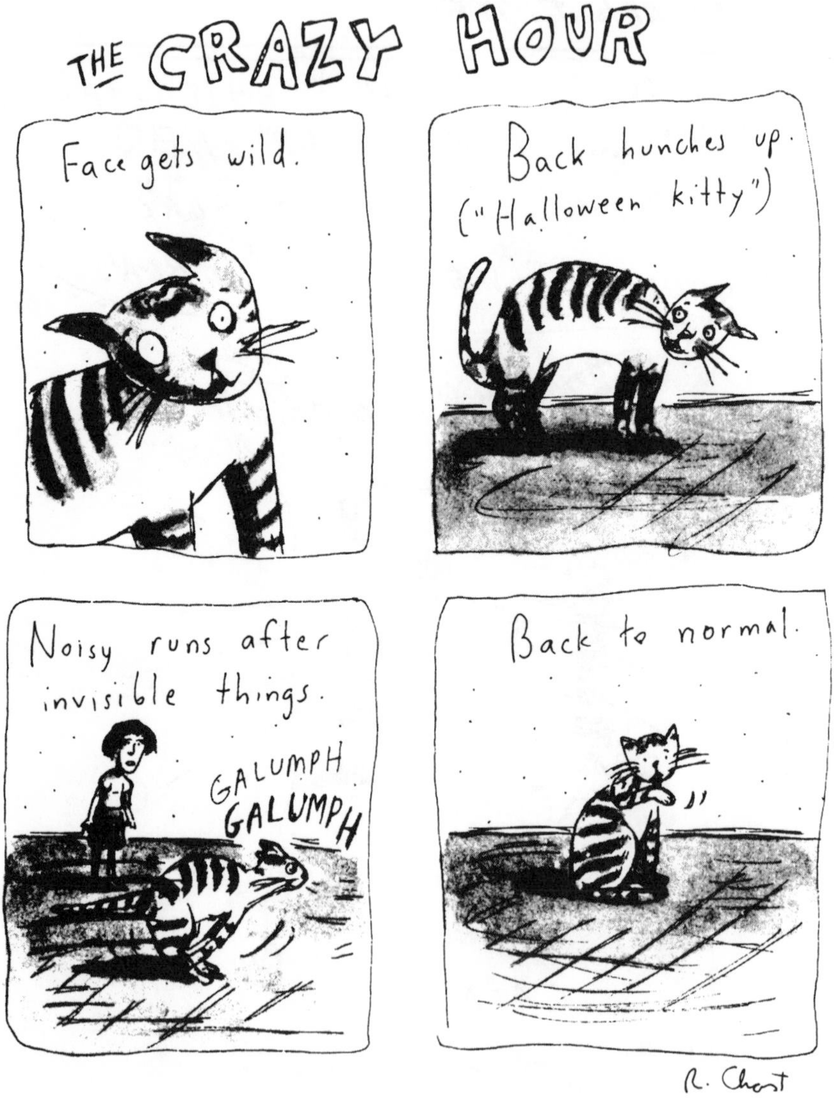
THE CRAZY HOUR
Face gets wild.
Back hunches up.
("Halloween kitty")
Noisy runs after invisible things.
GALUMPH
GALUMPH
Back to normal.
R. Chast

Diane Dimassa

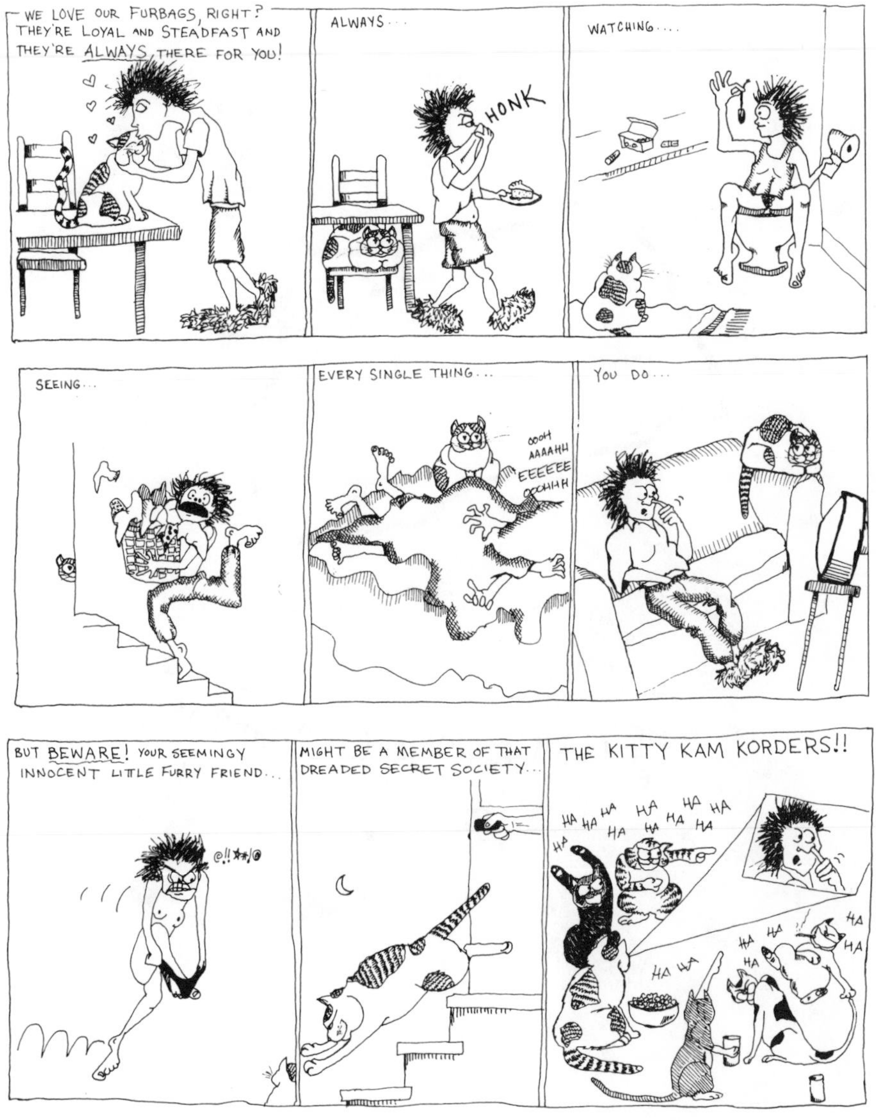
WE LOVE OUR FURBAGS, RIGHT? THEY'RE LOYAL AND STEADFAST AND THEY'RE ALWAYS THERE FOR YOU!
ALWAYS...
HONK
WATCHING....
SEEING...
EVERY SINGLE THING...
OOOH AAAAHH EEEEEE OOOHHH
YOU DO...
BUT BEWARE! YOUR SEEMINGY INNOCENT LITTLE FURRY FRIEND...
@!!*#!@
MIGHT BE A MEMBER OF THAT DREADED SECRET SOCIETY...
THE KITTY KAM KORDERS!!
HA HA HA HA HA HA HA HA HA HA HA HA
HA HA
HA HA HA HA HA

Anne Beidler

THE PURRIE HOME COMPANION

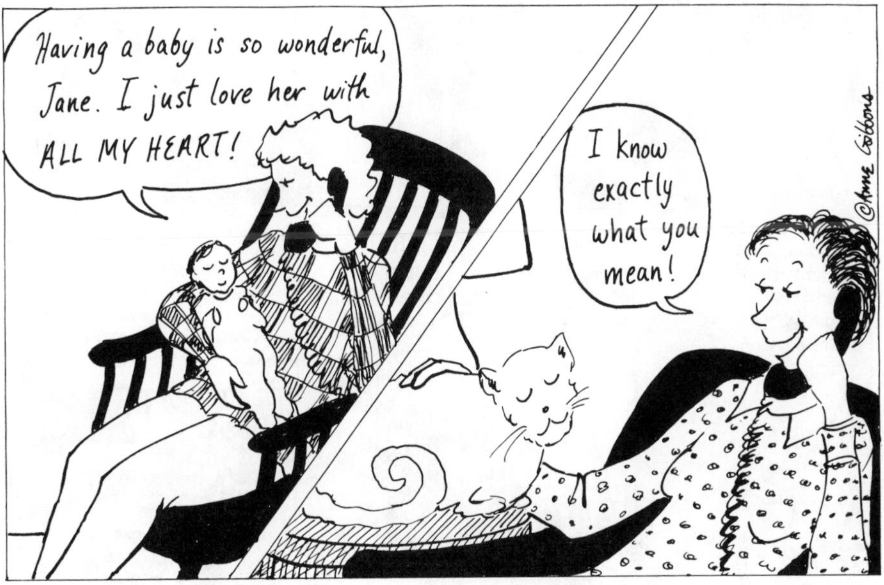
Having a baby is so wonderful, Jane. I just love her with ALL MY HEART!
I know exactly what you mean!
©Anne Gibbons

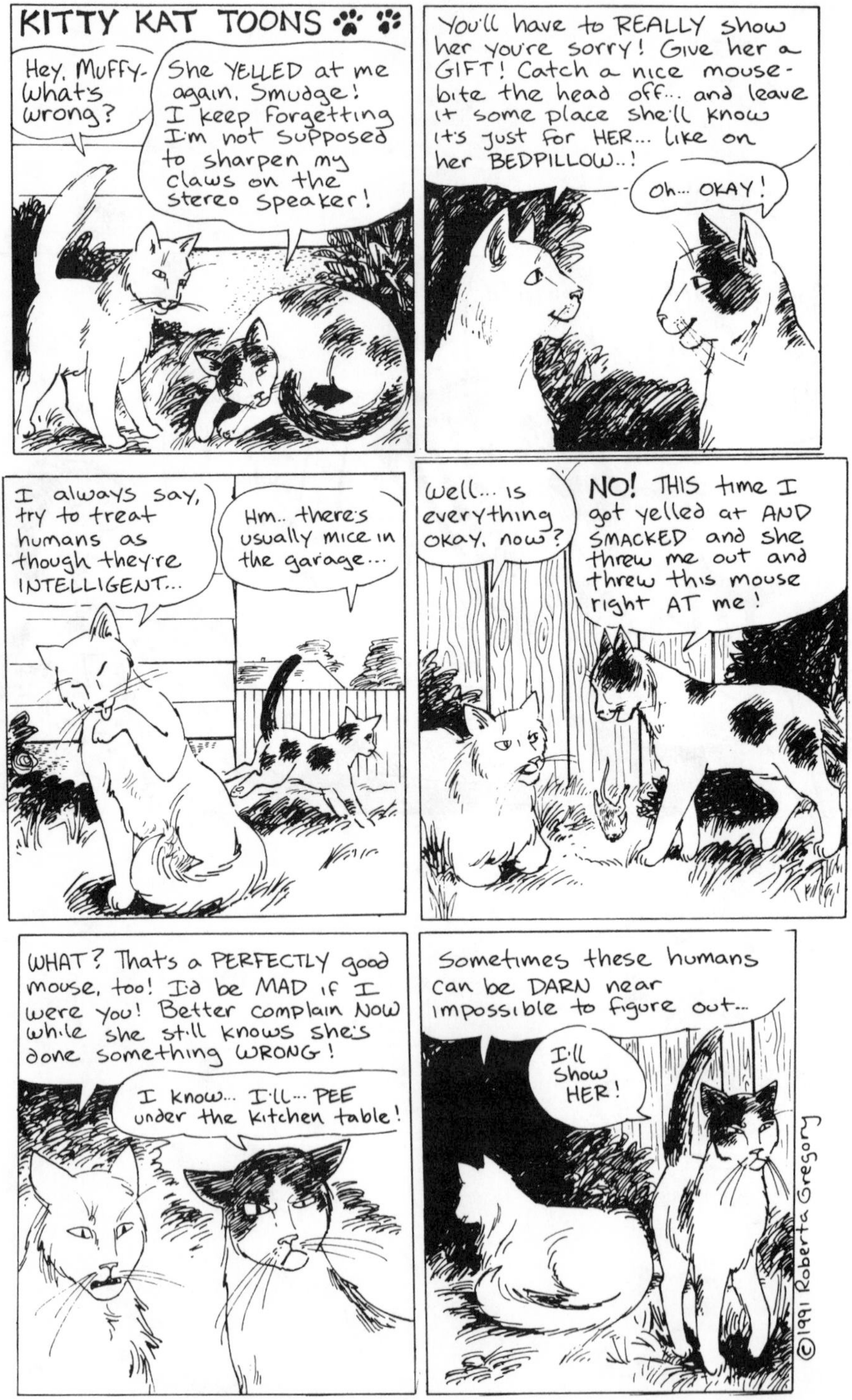
KITTY KAT TOONS
Hey, Muffy- What's wrong?
She YELLED at me again, Smudge! I keep forgetting I'm not supposed to sharpen my claws on the stereo speaker!
You'll have to REALLY show her you're sorry! Give her a GIFT! Catch a nice mouse- bite the head off... and leave it some place she'll know it's just for HER... like on her BEDPILLOW..!
Oh... OKAY!
I always say, try to treat humans as though they're INTELLIGENT...
Hm.. there's usually mice in the garage...
Well... is everything OKAY, now?
NO! THIS time I got yelled at AND SMACKED and she threw me out and threw this mouse right AT me!
WHAT? That's a PERFECTLY good mouse, too! I'd be MAD if I were you! Better complain NOW while she still knows she's done something WRONG!
I know... I'll... PEE under the kitchen table!
Sometimes these humans can be DARN near impossible to figure out...
I'll Show HER!
©1991 Roberta Gregory

Wendy Eastwood

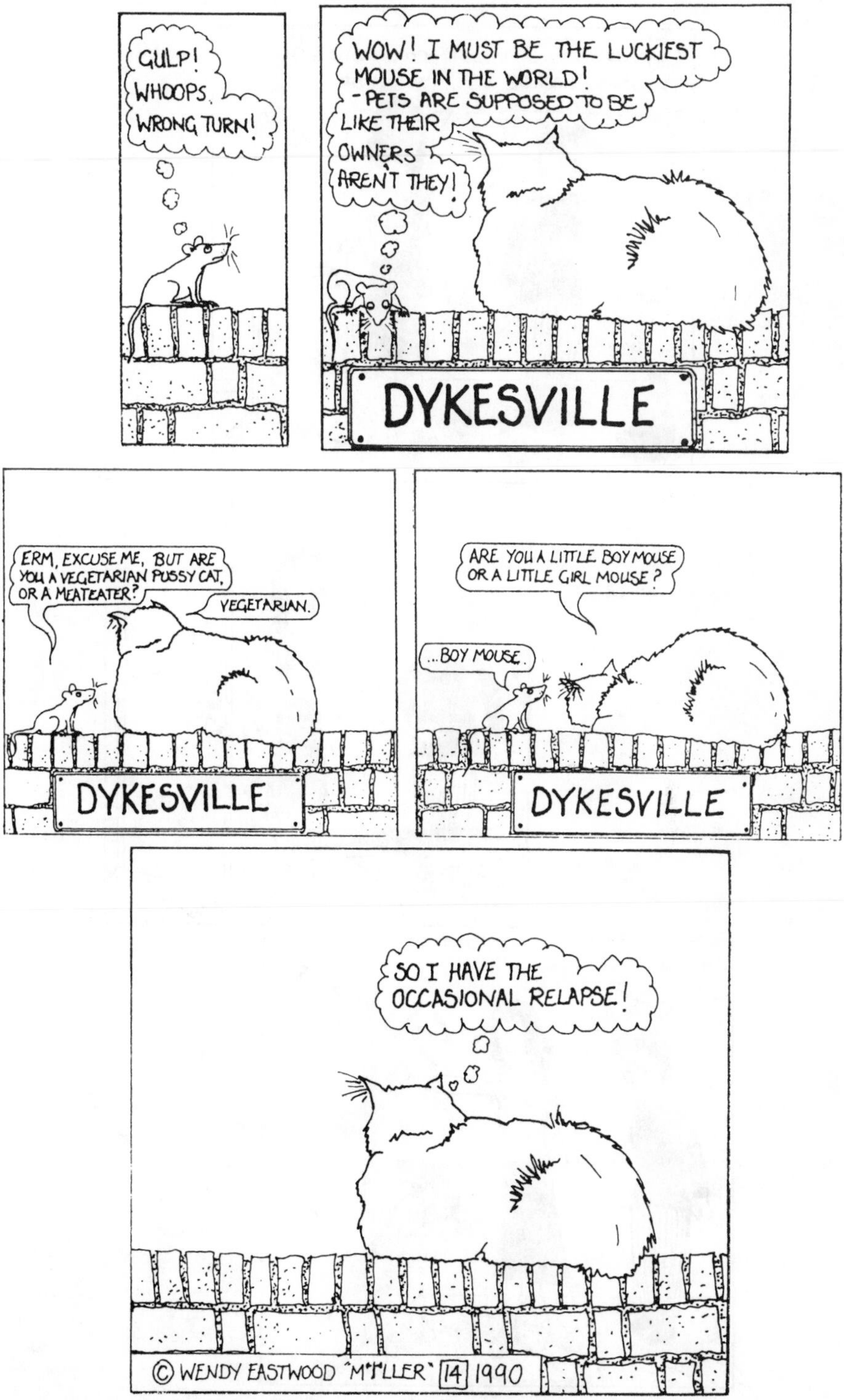
GULP! WHOOPS. WRONG TURN!
WOW! I MUST BE THE LUCKIEST MOUSE IN THE WORLD! - PETS ARE SUPPOSED TO BE LIKE THEIR OWNERS AREN'T THEY!
DYKESVILLE
ERM, EXCUSE ME, BUT ARE YOU A VEGETARIAN PUSSY CAT, OR A MEATEATER?
VEGETARIAN.
DYKESVILLE
ARE YOU A LITTLE BOY MOUSE OR A LITTLE GIRL MOUSE?
...BOY MOUSE.
DYKESVILLE
SO I HAVE THE OCCASIONAL RELAPSE!
© WENDY EASTWOOD "M*LLER" 14 1990

Roberta Gregory

Cupcake's an "inside" cat. she's happy to stay INSIDE all the time...
I SEE!
SLAM!

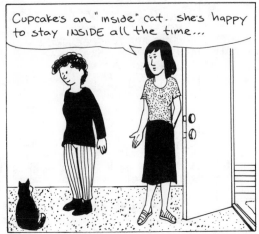

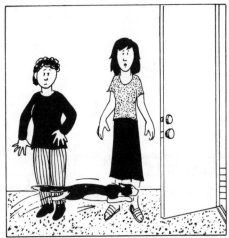

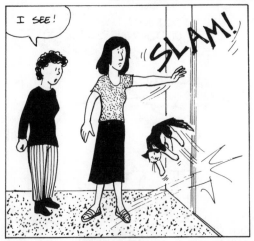

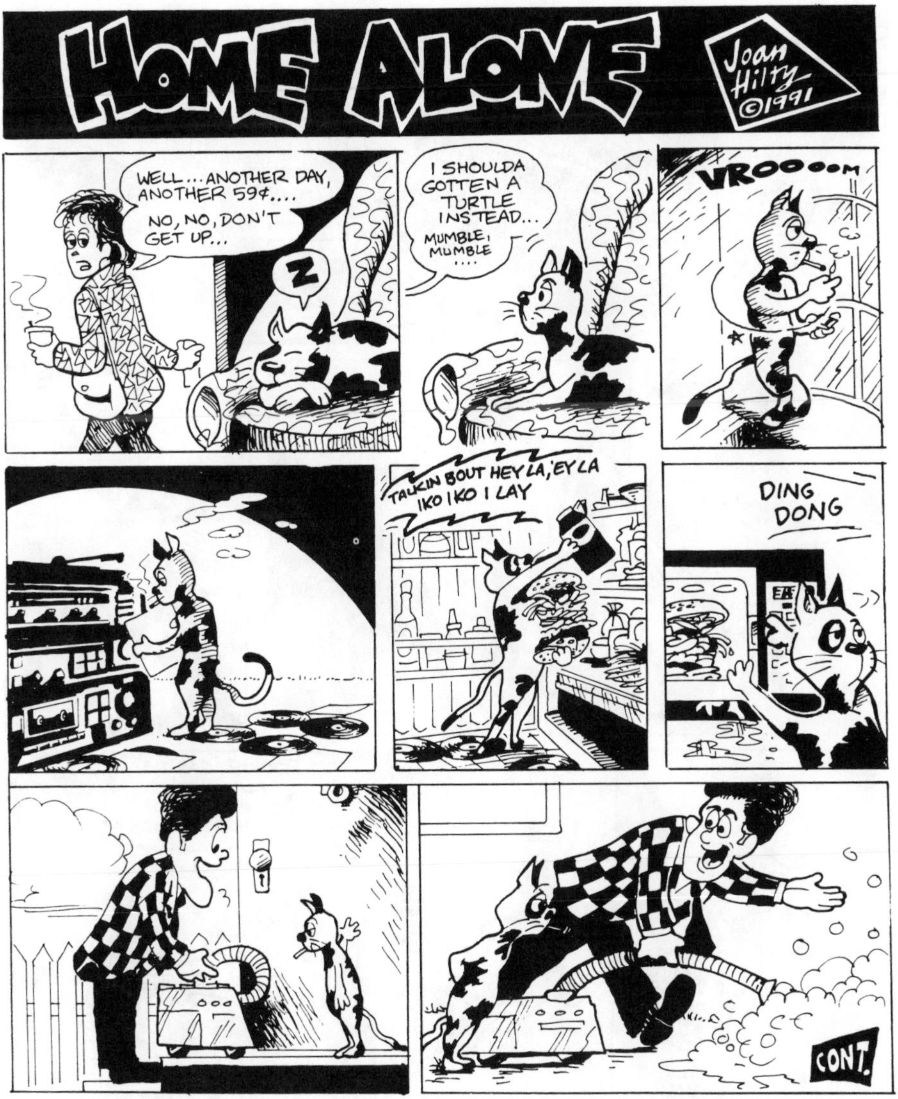
HOME ALONE
Joan Hilty ©1991
WELL... ANOTHER DAY, ANOTHER 59¢....
NO, NO, DON'T GET UP...
Z
I SHOULDA GOTTEN A TURTLE INSTEAD...
MUMBLE, MUMBLE ....
VROOOoom
TALKIN BOUT HEY LA, 'EY LA IKO IKO I LAY
DING DONG
CONT.

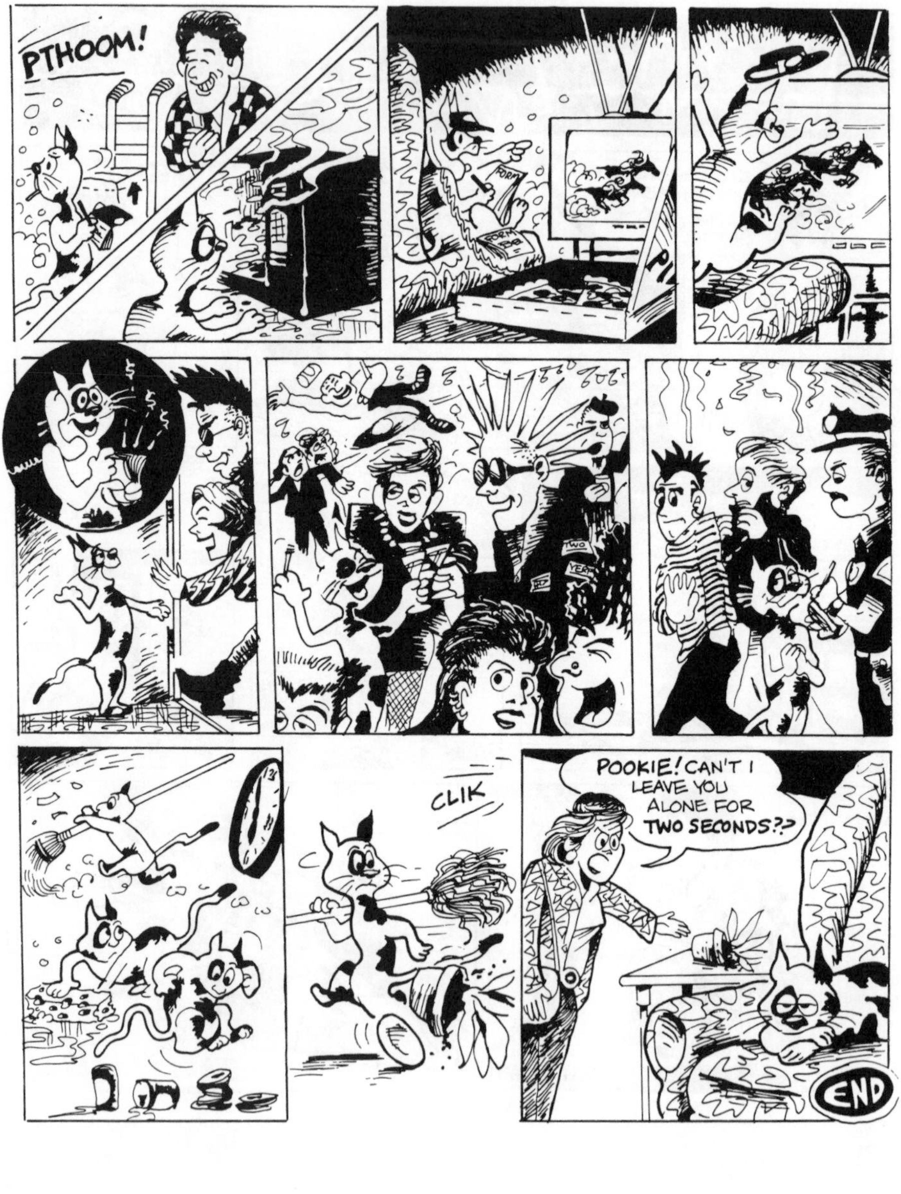
PTHOOM!
FORM
TWO
YEARS
CLIK
POOKIE! CAN'T I LEAVE YOU ALONE FOR TWO SECONDS?!?
END

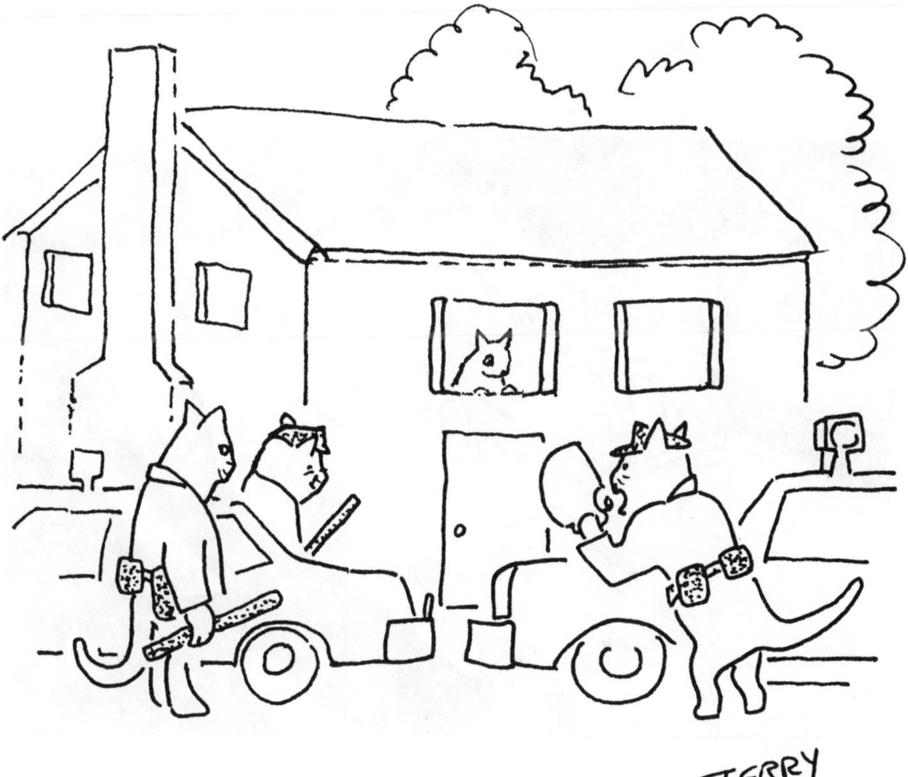
TERRY

All right, Whiskers, come out
with your claws retracted.

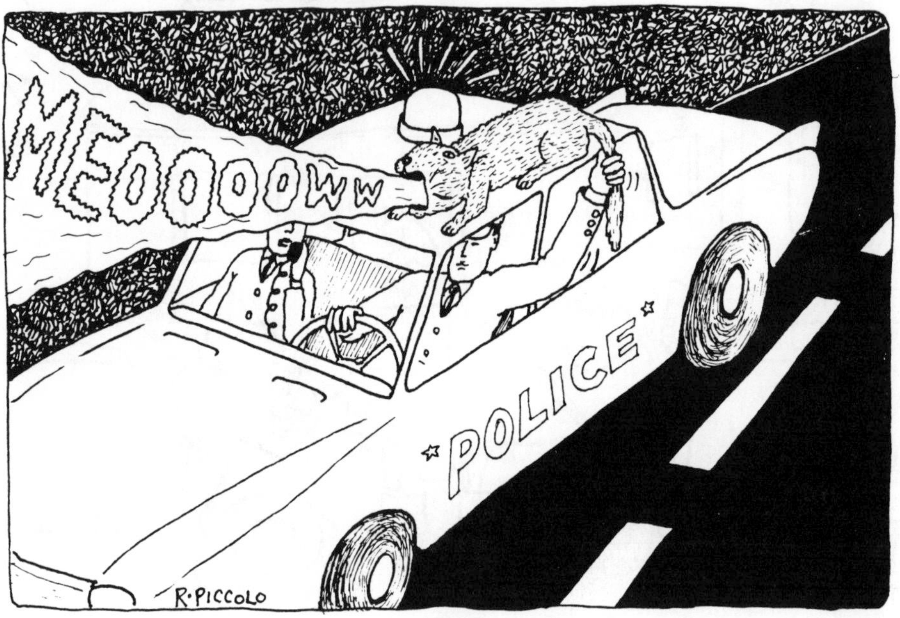
MEOOOOWW
POLICE
R. PICCOLO

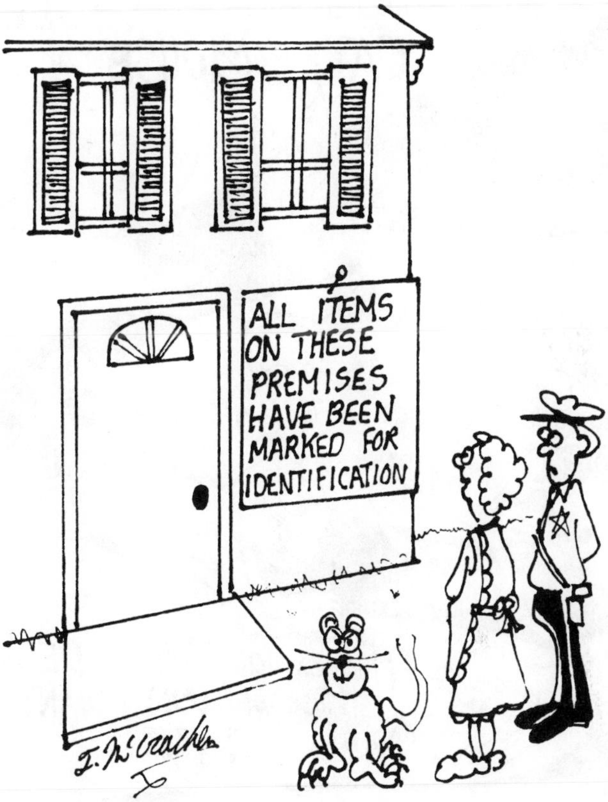
ALL ITEMS ON THESE PREMISES HAVE BEEN MARKED FOR IDENTIFICATION
T. McCracken

"MY CAT SPRAYED EVERYTHING IN THE HOUSE."

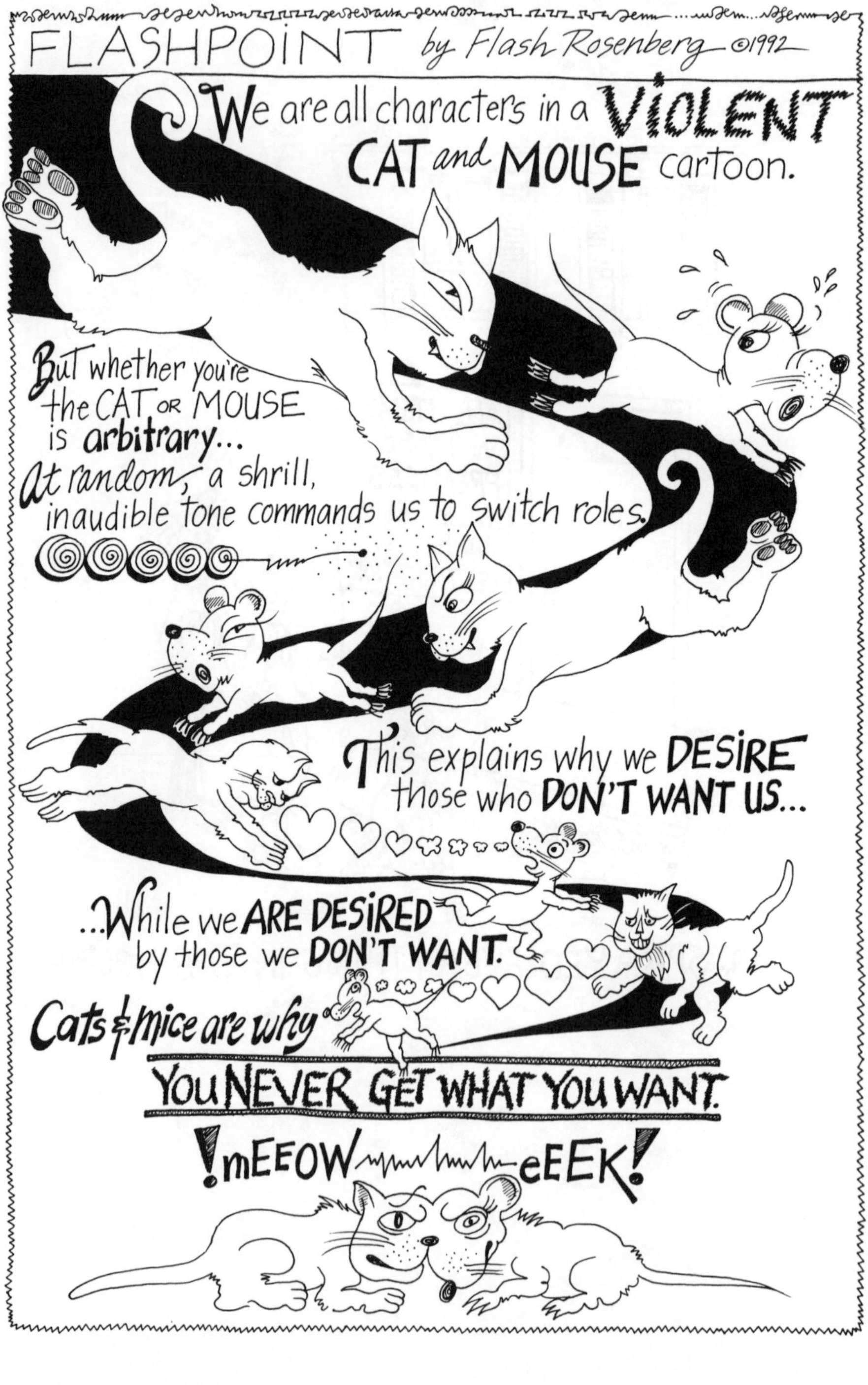
FLASHPOINT by Flash Rosenberg ©1992
We are all characters in a VIOLENT CAT and MOUSE cartoon.
But whether you're the CAT OR MOUSE is arbitrary...
At random, a shrill, inaudible tone commands us to switch roles.
This explains why we DESIRE those who DON'T WANT US...
...While we ARE DESIRED by those we DON'T WANT.
Cats & Mice are why
YOU NEVER GET WHAT YOU WANT.
!mEEOW eEEK!

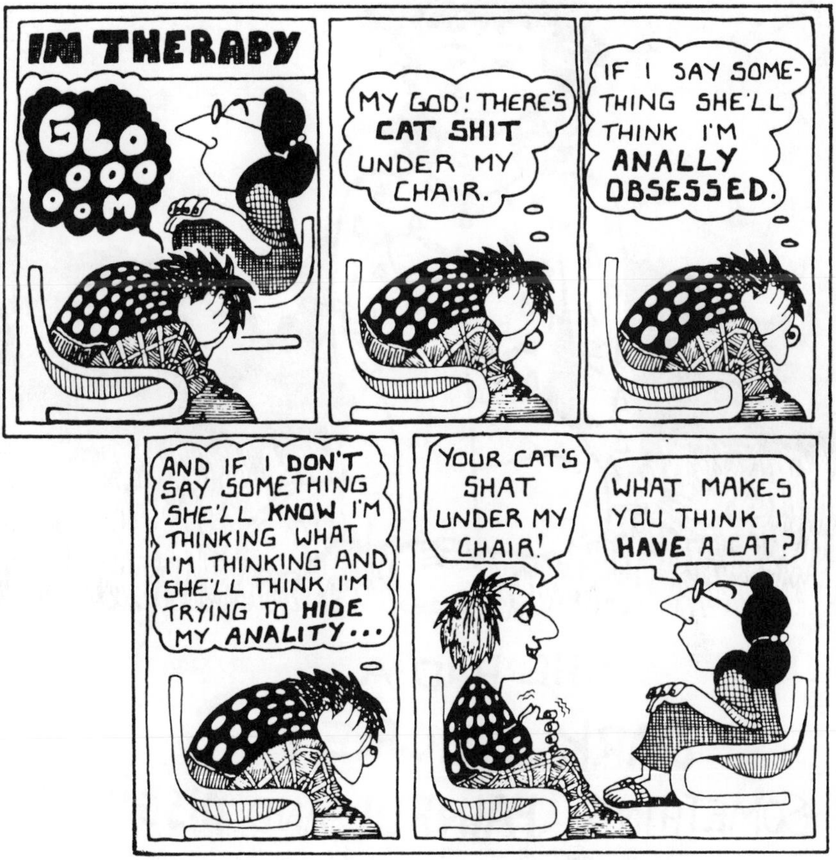
IN THERAPY
GLOOOOOOM
MY GOD! THERE'S CAT SHIT UNDER MY CHAIR.
IF I SAY SOMETHING SHE'LL THINK I'M ANALLY OBSESSED.
AND IF I DON'T SAY SOMETHING SHE'LL KNOW I'M THINKING WHAT I'M THINKING AND SHE'LL THINK I'M TRYING TO HIDE MY ANALITY...
YOUR CAT'S SHAT UNDER MY CHAIR!
WHAT MAKES YOU THINK I HAVE A CAT?

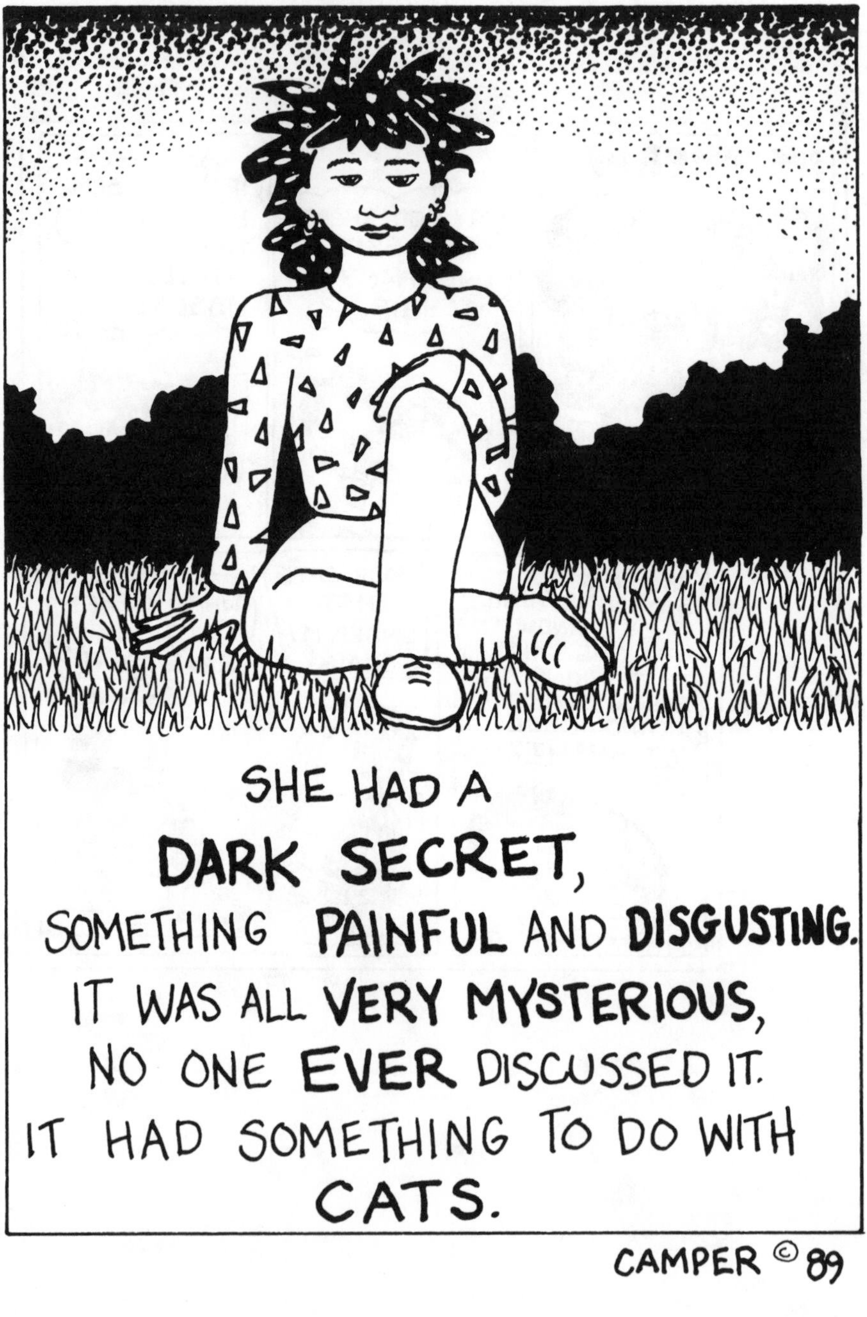
SHE HAD A
DARK SECRET,
SOMETHING PAINFUL AND DISGUSTING.
IT WAS ALL VERY MYSTERIOUS,
NO ONE EVER DISCUSSED IT.
IT HAD SOMETHING TO DO WITH
CATS.
CAMPER © 89

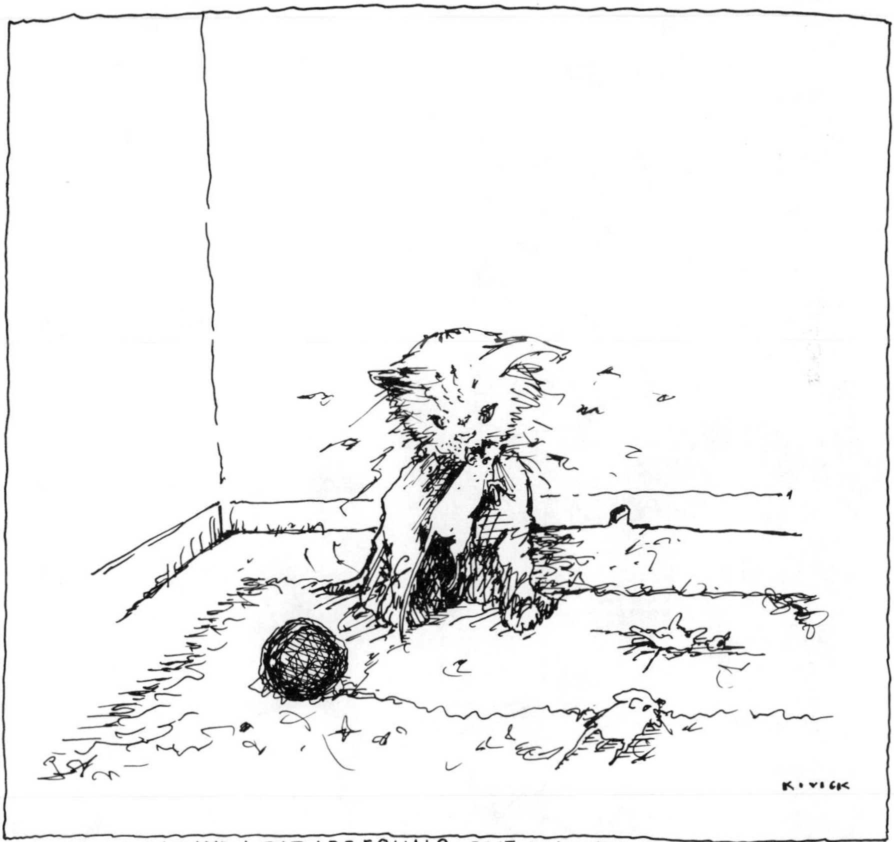
KOVICK

MORALLY A CAT AND A RAT ARE EQUALS, BUT WHICH ONE WOULD YOU RATHER HAVE IN BED WITH YOU?

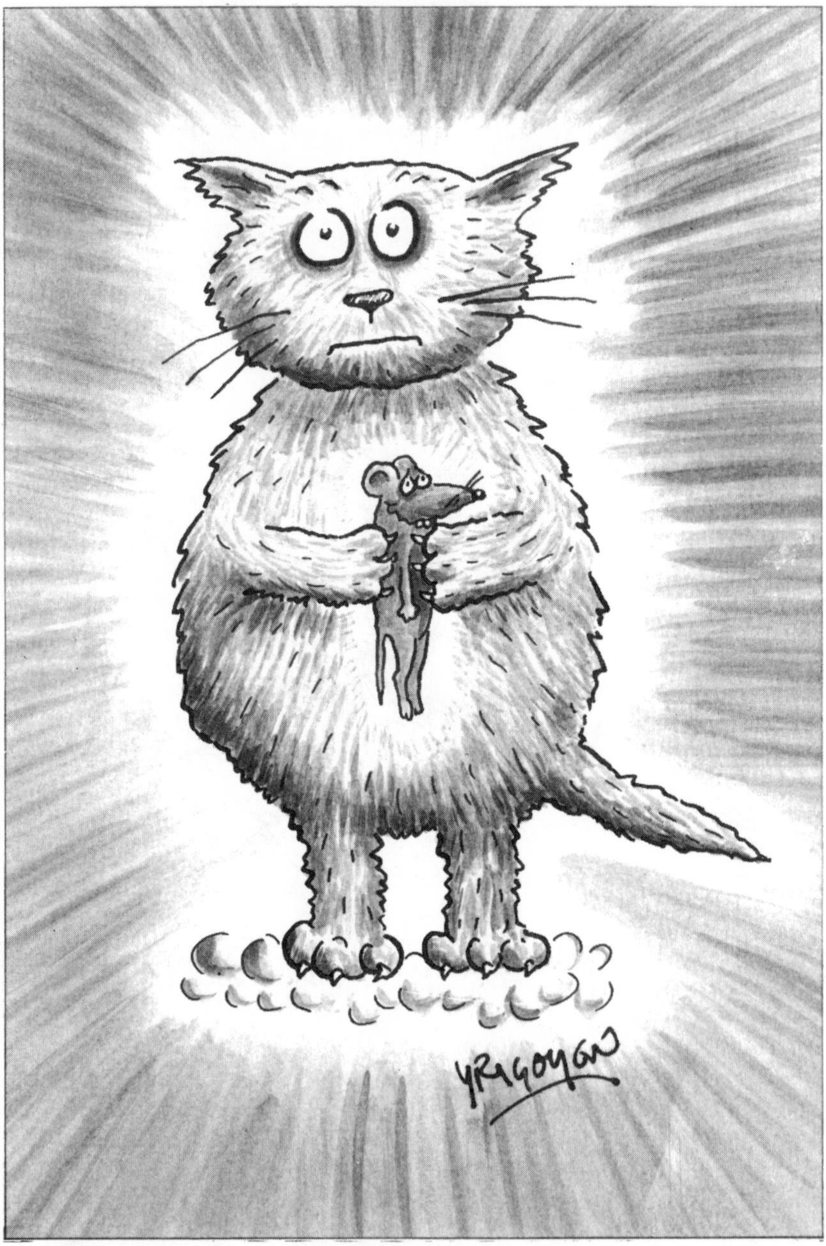
YRIGOYEN

FOR A MOMENT THEY WERE FROZEN IN TIME
CALLING THE CAT A LAPSED VEGETARIAN WAS A CALCULATED RISK, AND NEITHER KNEW IF IT WOULD BRING REVENGE OR REMORSE....

Look Dukie, I brought you a friend

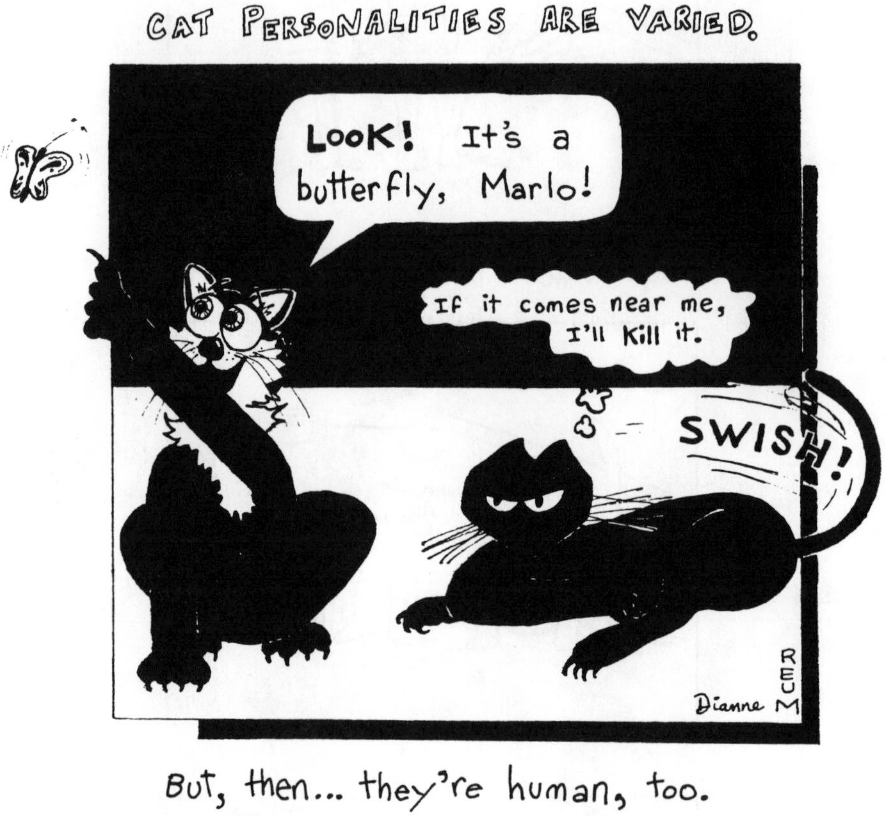
CAT PERSONALITIES ARE VARIED.
LOOK! It's a butterfly, Marlo!
If it comes near me, I'll Kill it.
SWISH!
Dianne REUM
But, then... they're human, too.

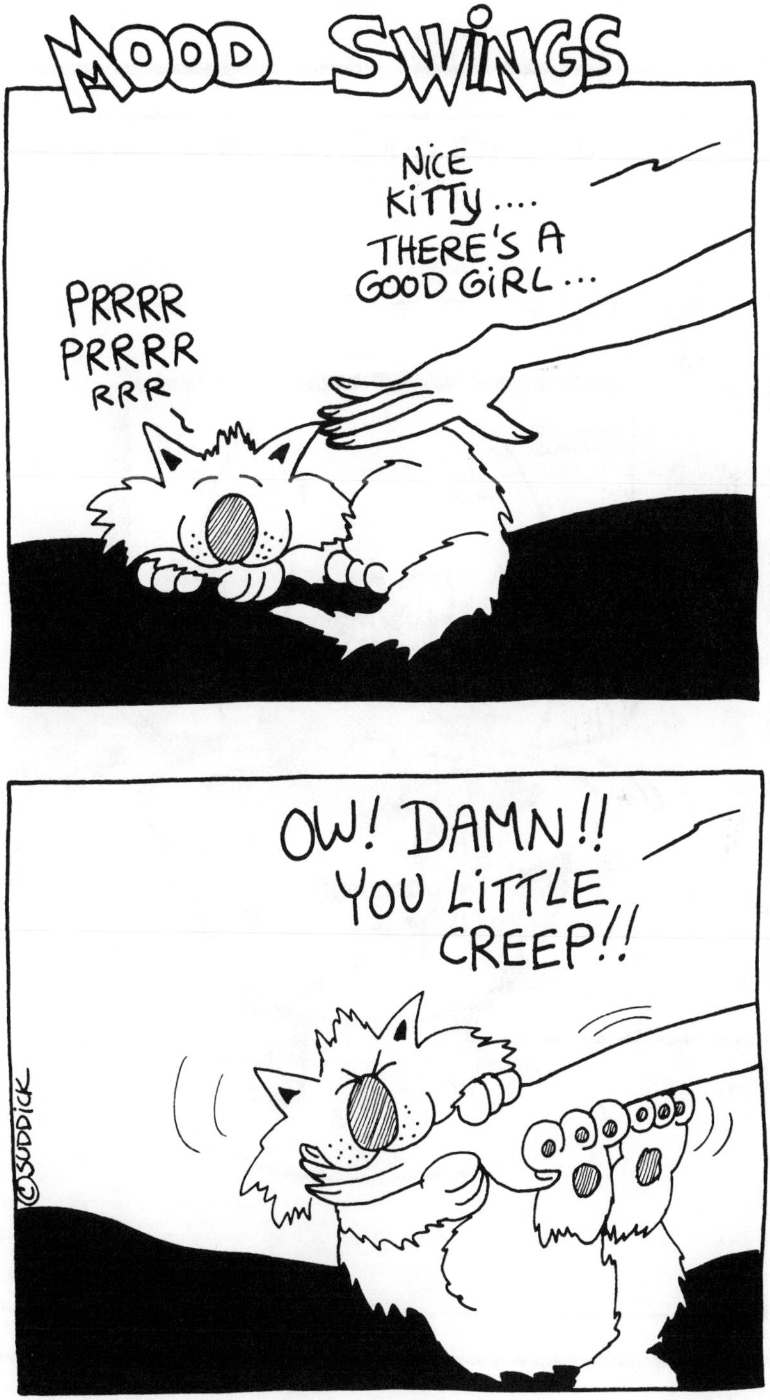
MOOD SWINGS
NICE KITTY.... THERE'S A GOOD GIRL...
PRRRR PRRRRR RRR
OW! DAMN!! YOU LITTLE CREEP!!
©SUDDICK

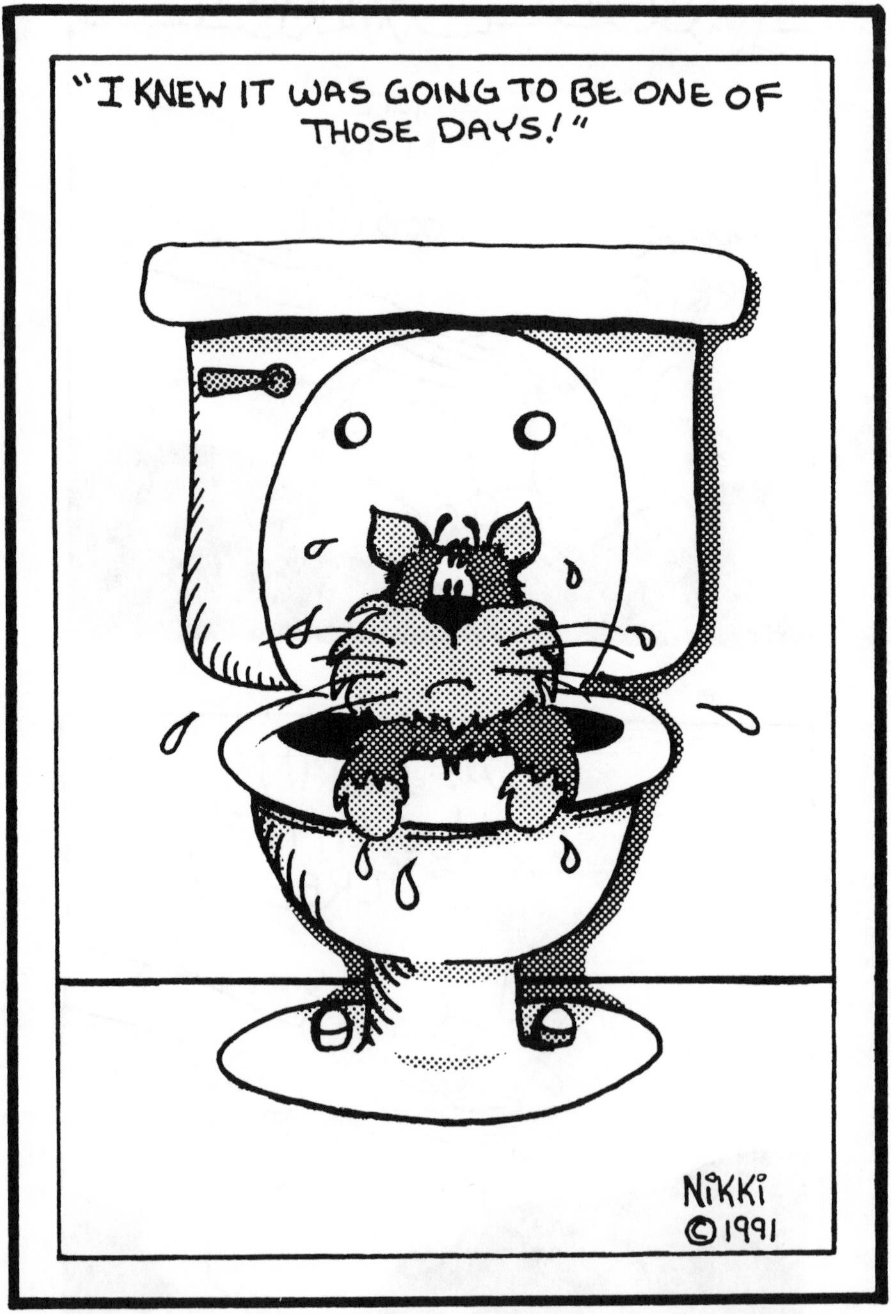
"I KNEW IT WAS GOING TO BE ONE OF THOSE DAYS!"
NIKKI
©1991

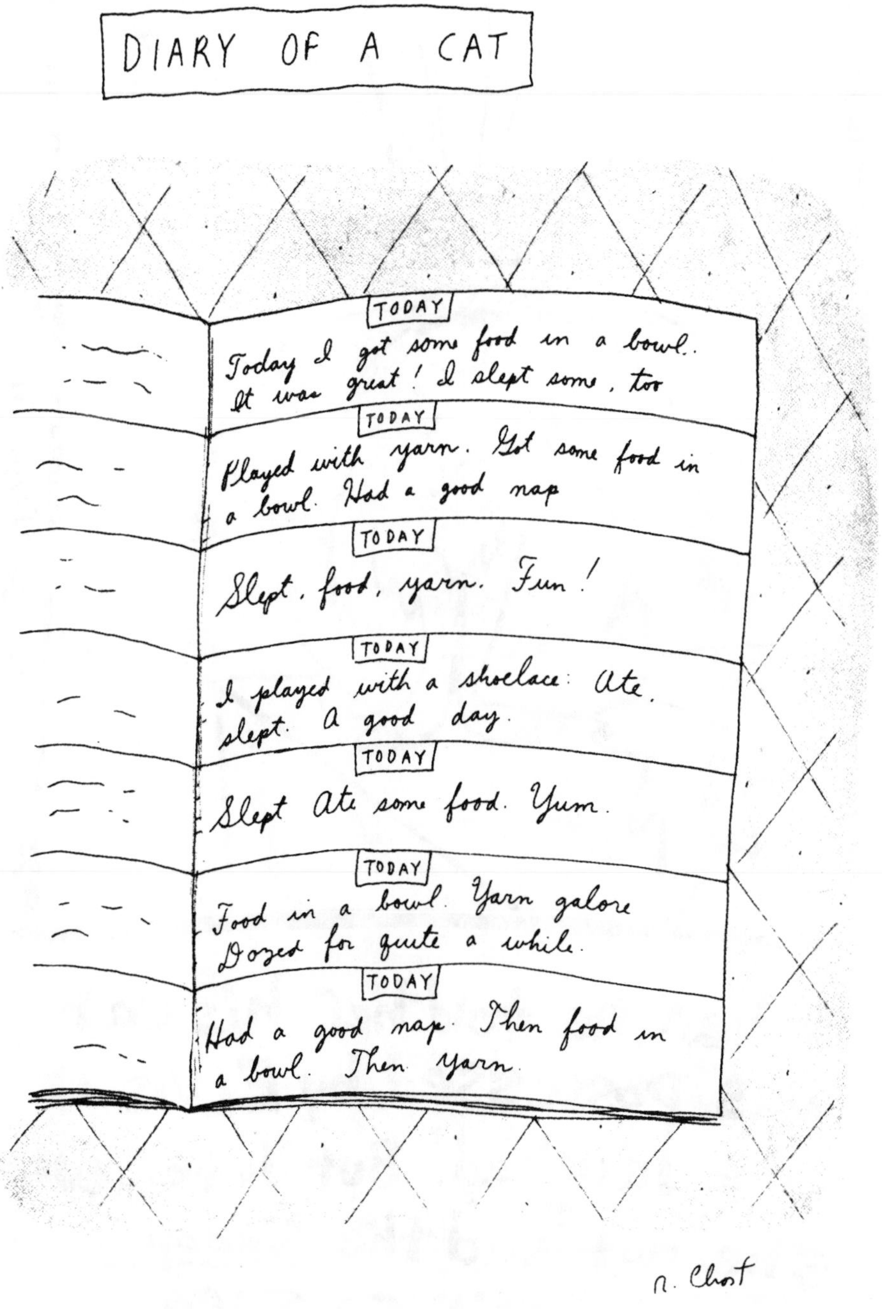
DIARY OF A CAT
TODAY
Today I got some food in a bowl. It was great! I slept some, too
TODAY
Played with yarn. Got some food in a bowl. Had a good nap
TODAY
Slept, food, yarn. Fun!
TODAY
I played with a shoelace. Ate. slept. A good day.
TODAY
Slept Ate some food. Yum.
TODAY
Food in a bowl. Yarn galore Dozed for quite a while.
TODAY
Had a good nap. Then food in a bowl. Then yarn.
R. Chast

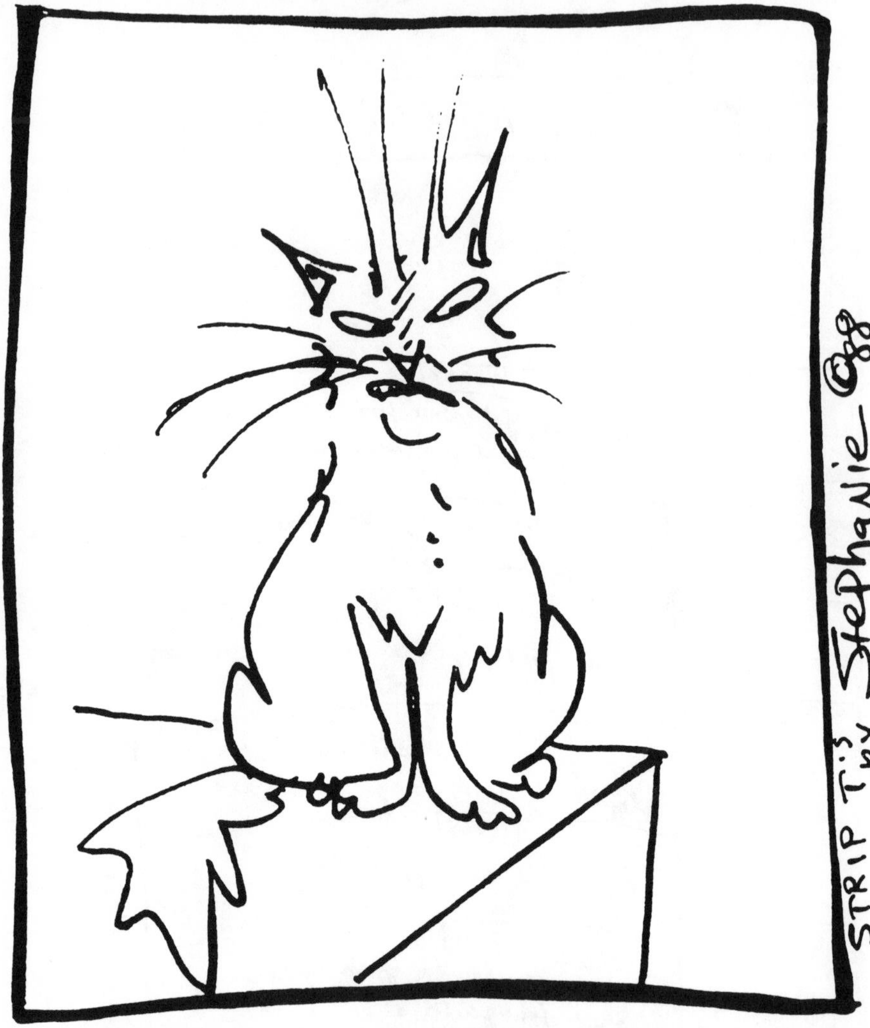
Stephanie ©88

When he told her his cat was possessed by ELVIS... She laughed! But later, when she noticed the sneer... She wasn't so sure...

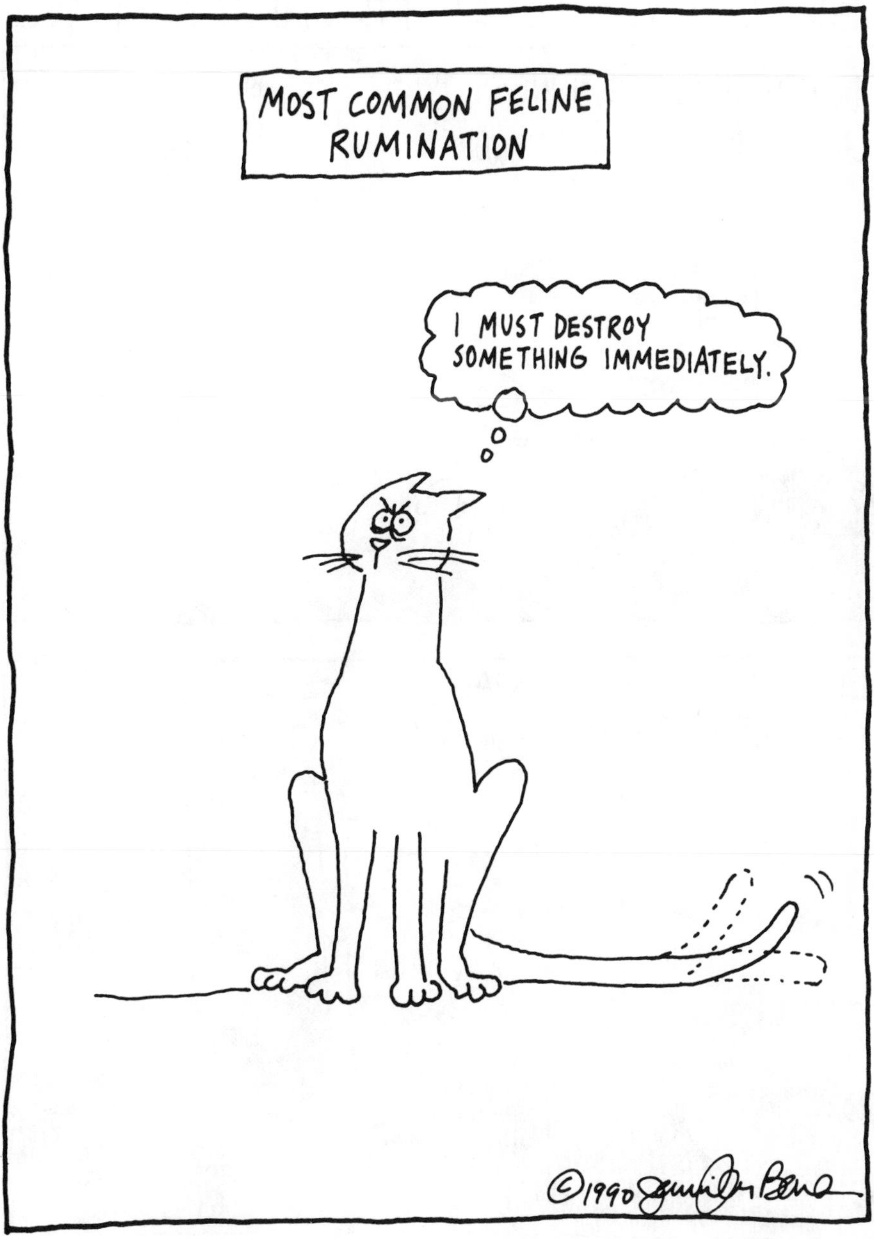
MOST COMMON FELINE RUMINATION
I MUST DESTROY SOMETHING IMMEDIATELY.
©1990 Jennifer Berman

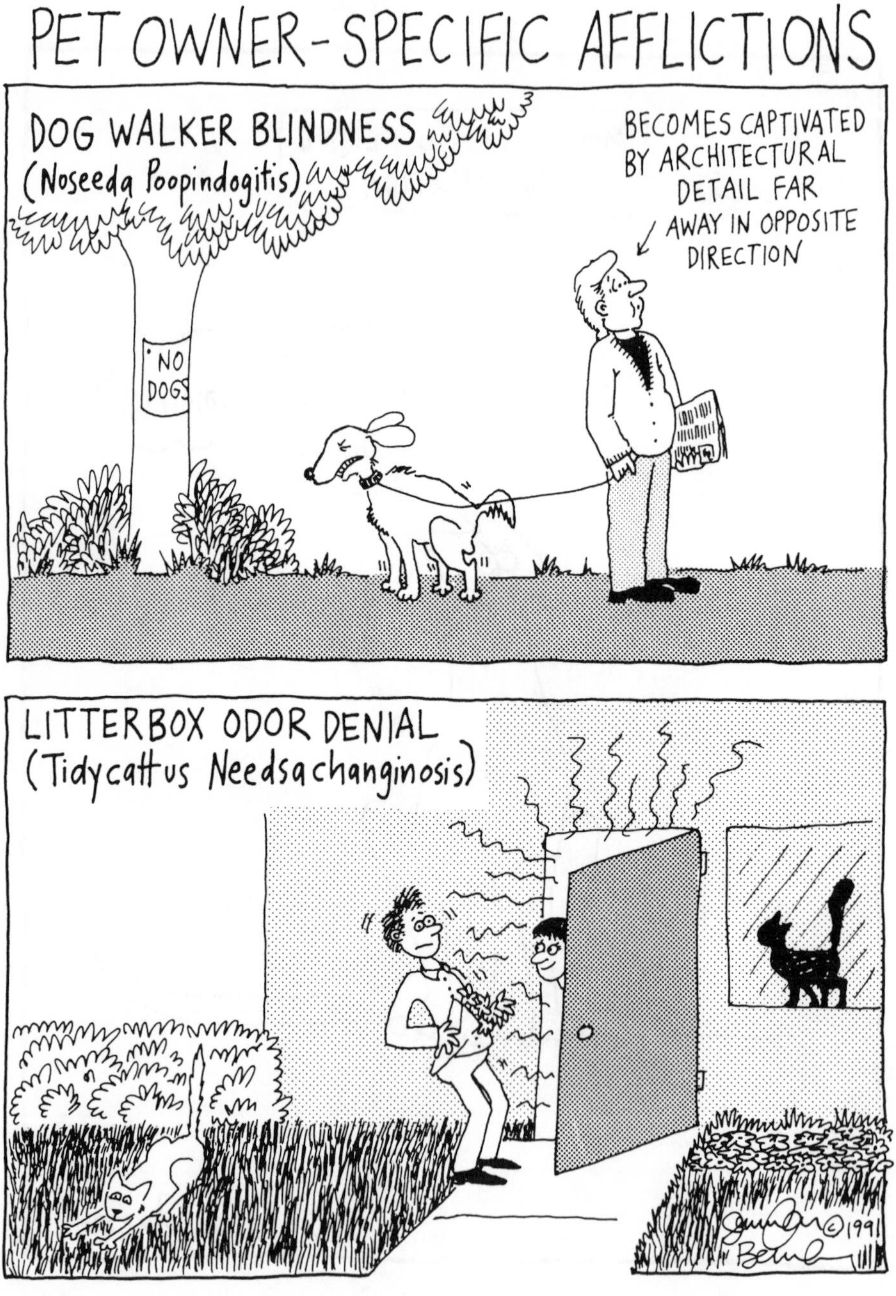
PET OWNER-SPECIFIC AFFLICTIONS
DOG WALKER BLINDNESS
(Noseeda Poopindogitis)
BECOMES CAPTIVATED BY ARCHITECTURAL DETAIL FAR AWAY IN OPPOSITE DIRECTION
NO DOGS
LITTERBOX ODOR DENIAL
(Tidycattus Needsachanginosis)
©1991 Berman

STONEWALL RIOTS

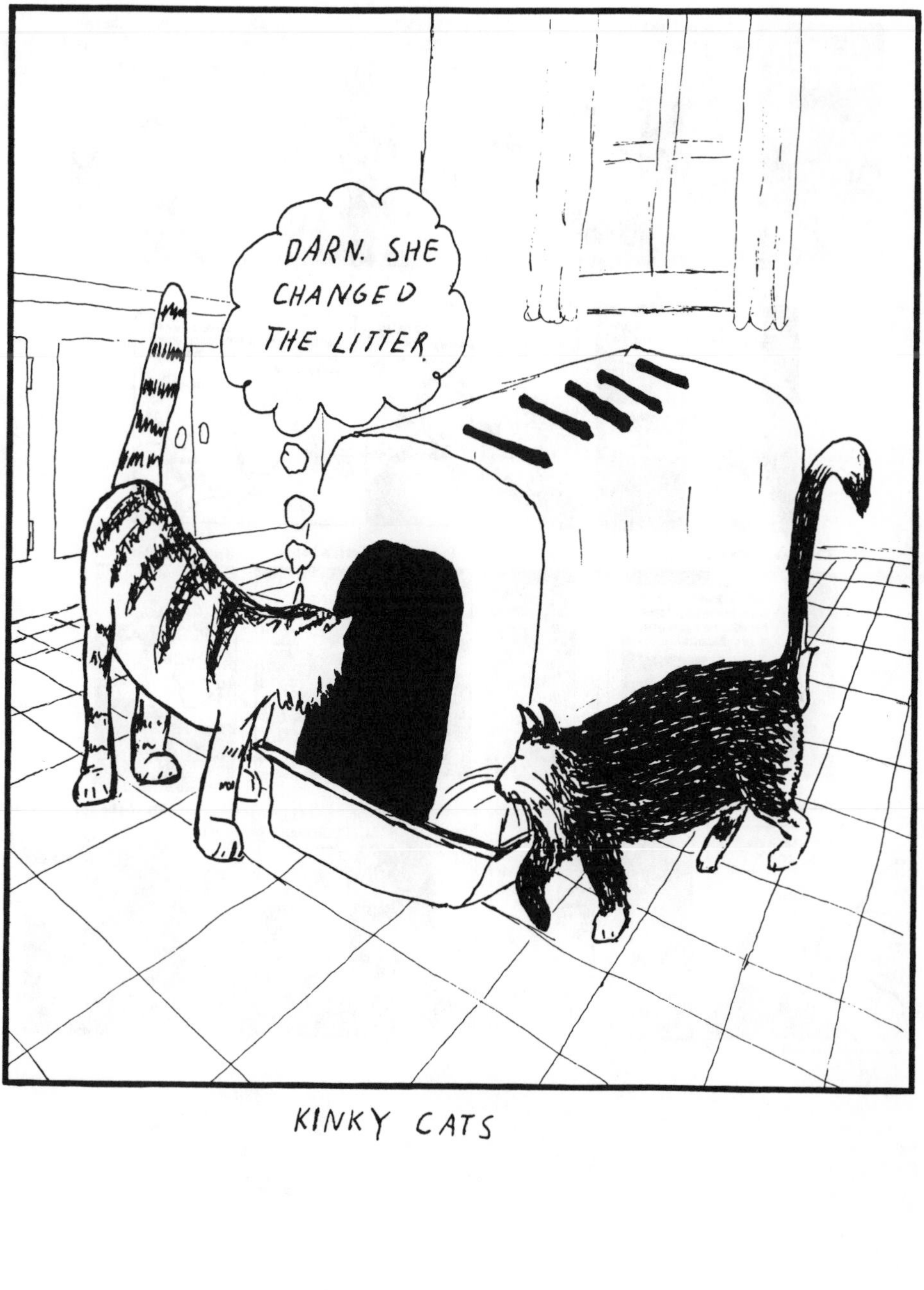
DARN. SHE CHANGED THE LITTER

KINKY CATS

Posy Simmonds

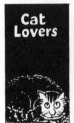

Cat Lovers
The cat sat on the mat.
Back to the flat, come Pat and Jack.
First things first...where's that bloody cat of yours?
Oh DON'T call him that!
Jack hates the cat.
Well, I'm sorry...but it BIT me last time I was here, remember?
The cat hates Jack.
Oh Jack! Pussy's just not used to you, yet! He's jealous....
Just keep him out of my way, that's all...
Pat loves the cat.
Oh listen! You mustn't be nasty about my poor puddy-tat! He's a lovely boy..he really is!
Oh yes?
You don't know what a sweet, faithful friend he's been to me all these years....ever since he was a tiny kitty..!
The cat loves Pat.
He's a Scorpio...little sting in the tail, sometimes...he's just a tiny bit jealous......
Pat sat on Jack's lap.
Jack pets Pat.
Jack and Pat want a nap.
Shall we... er...?
mMm
Scram, cat, scram!
Oh God!
Drat the cat!
The cat sh*t on the mat...

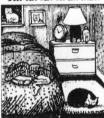

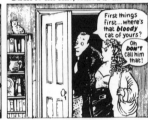

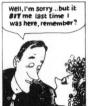

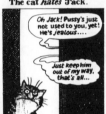

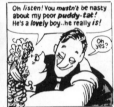

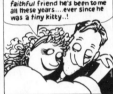

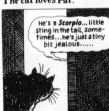

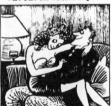

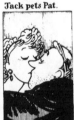

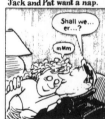

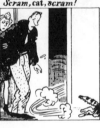

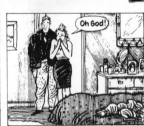

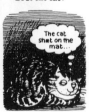

© Posy Simmonds 1984

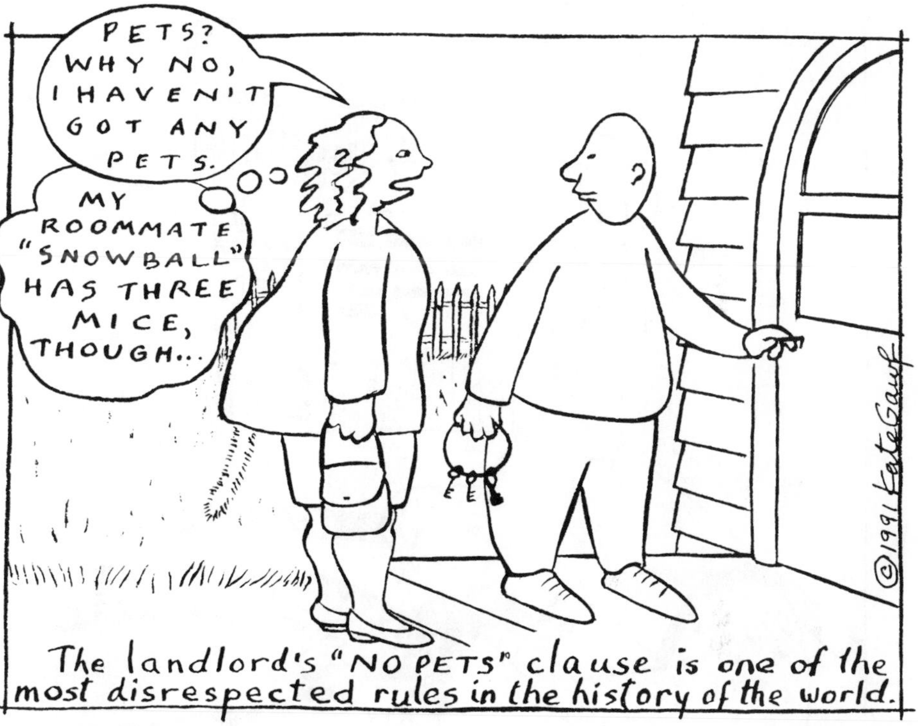
PETS? WHY NO, I HAVEN'T GOT ANY PETS.
MY ROOMMATE "SNOWBALL" HAS THREE MICE, THOUGH...
©1991 Kate Gawf
The landlord's "NO PETS" clause is one of the most disrespected rules in the history of the world.

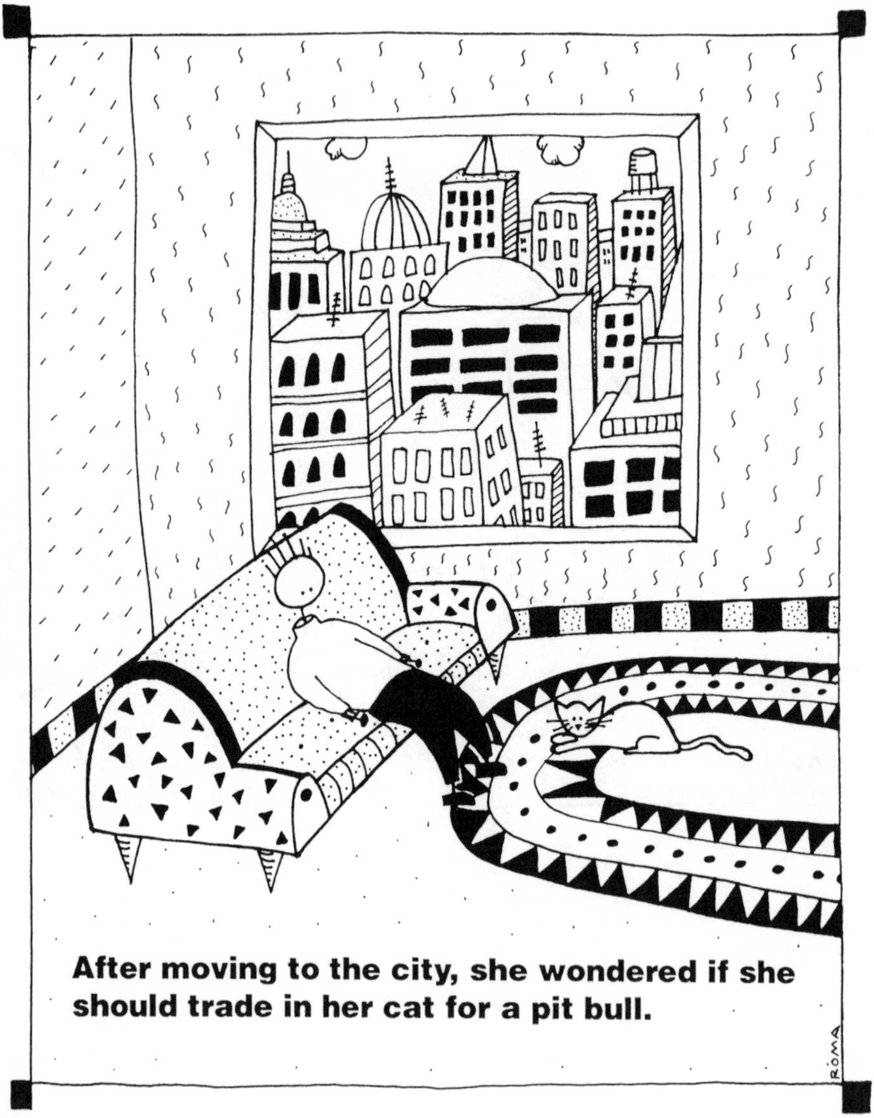
ROMA

After moving to the city, she wondered if she should trade in her cat for a pit bull.

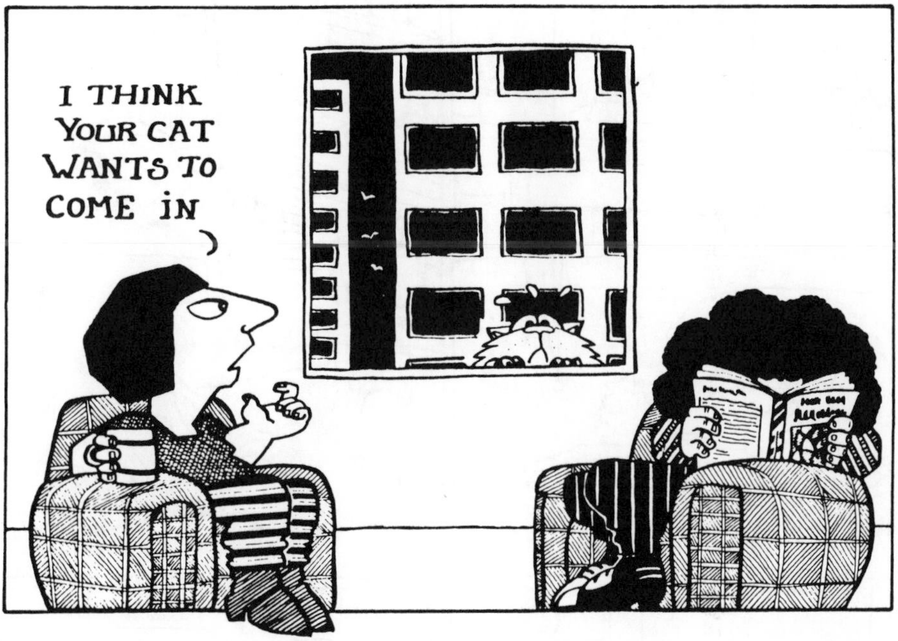
I THINK YOUR CAT WANTS TO COME IN

Marian Henley

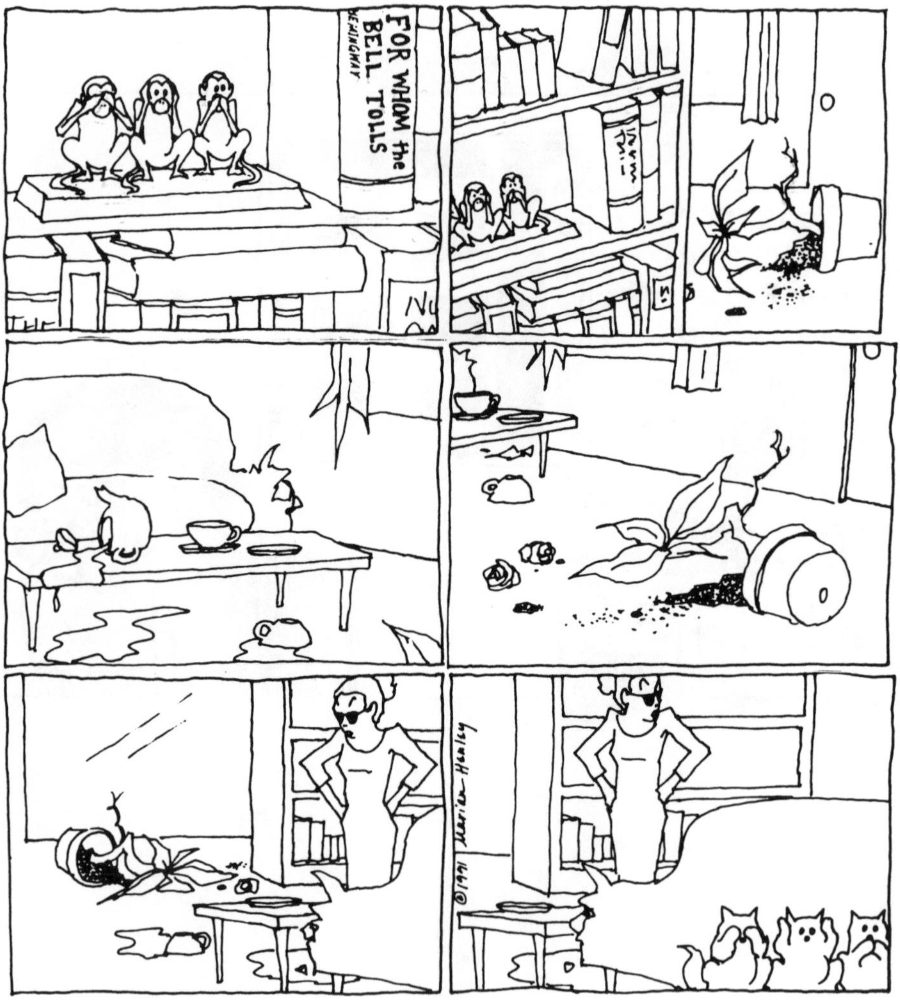
FOR WHOM the
BELL TOLLS
HEMINGWAY
©1991 Marian Henley

RECENTLY DISCOVERED SCIENTIFIC EVIDENCE REVEALS THAT CERTAIN CAT BEHAVIORS ACTUALLY CARRY A SPECIFIC MESSAGE...

SO PAY ATTENTION!
BOOPSIE MAY BE TRYING TO TELL YOU SOMETHING!!!

A PRIMER FOR THE NOVICE...
A CHECKLIST FOR THE JADED...

©1991 DIANE DiMASSA

"I do not wish to be petted, touch me and bleed."

"I don't like that kind."

"oh, is my catbox dirty? I didn't even notice."

"you did something that upset me. now guess what it is."

"OK, pet me now."

"i'm in heat, do something!"

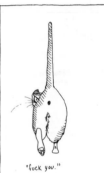

"fuck you."

"get up."

"you're not trying....."

ONE MILLIMETER

"I love living here."

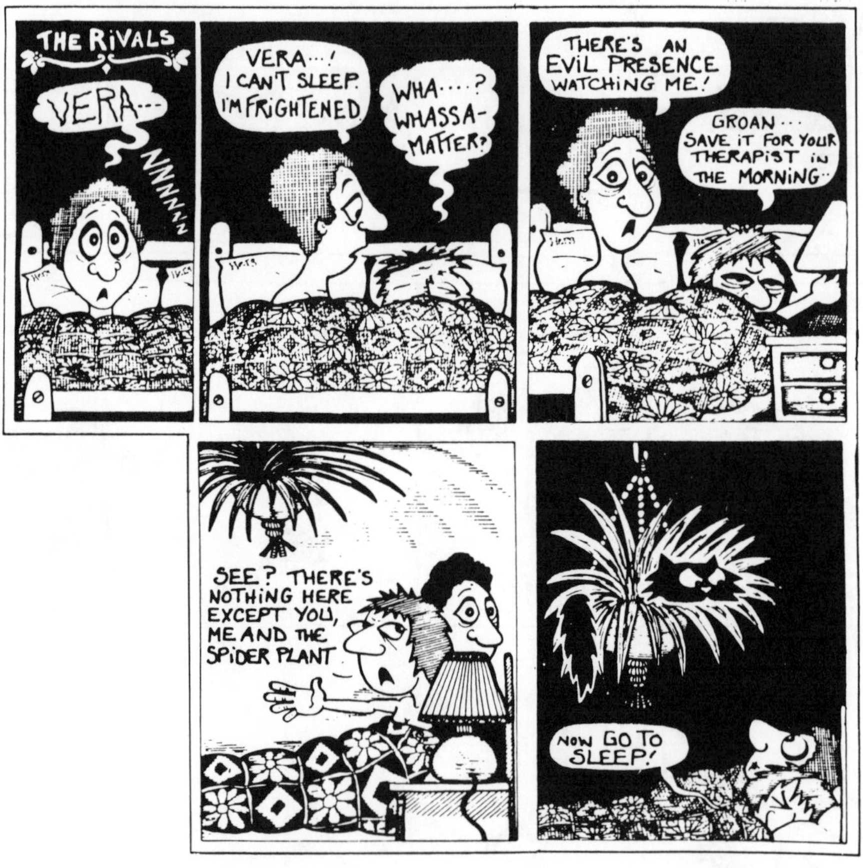
THE RIVALS
VERA...
ZZZZZZ
VERA...! I CAN'T SLEEP. I'M FRIGHTENED.
WHA....? WHASSA-MATTER?
THERE'S AN EVIL PRESENCE WATCHING ME!
GROAN... SAVE IT FOR YOUR THERAPIST IN THE MORNING..
SEE? THERE'S NOTHING HERE EXCEPT YOU, ME AND THE SPIDER PLANT.
NOW GO TO SLEEP!

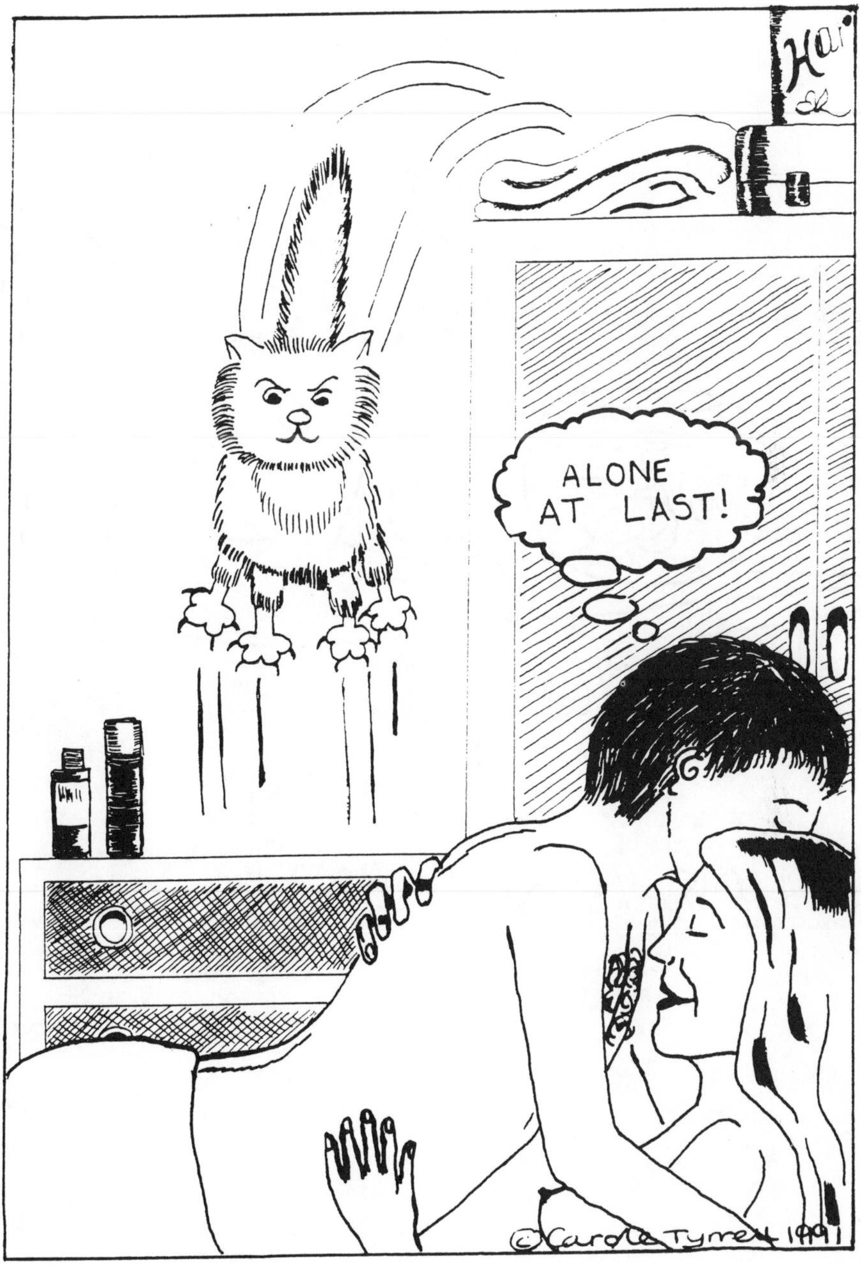
ALONE AT LAST!
©Carole Tyrrell 1991

"LOOK. A SUSHI BAR."

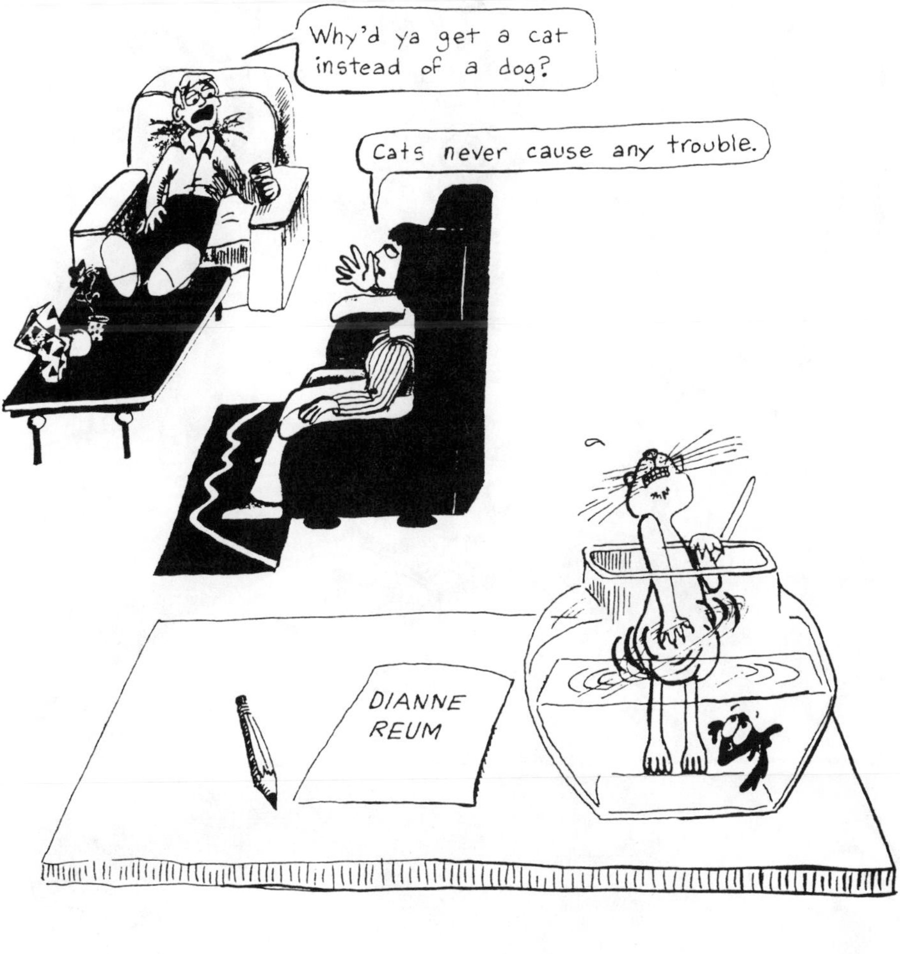
Why'd ya get a cat instead of a dog?
Cats never cause any trouble.
DIANNE REUM

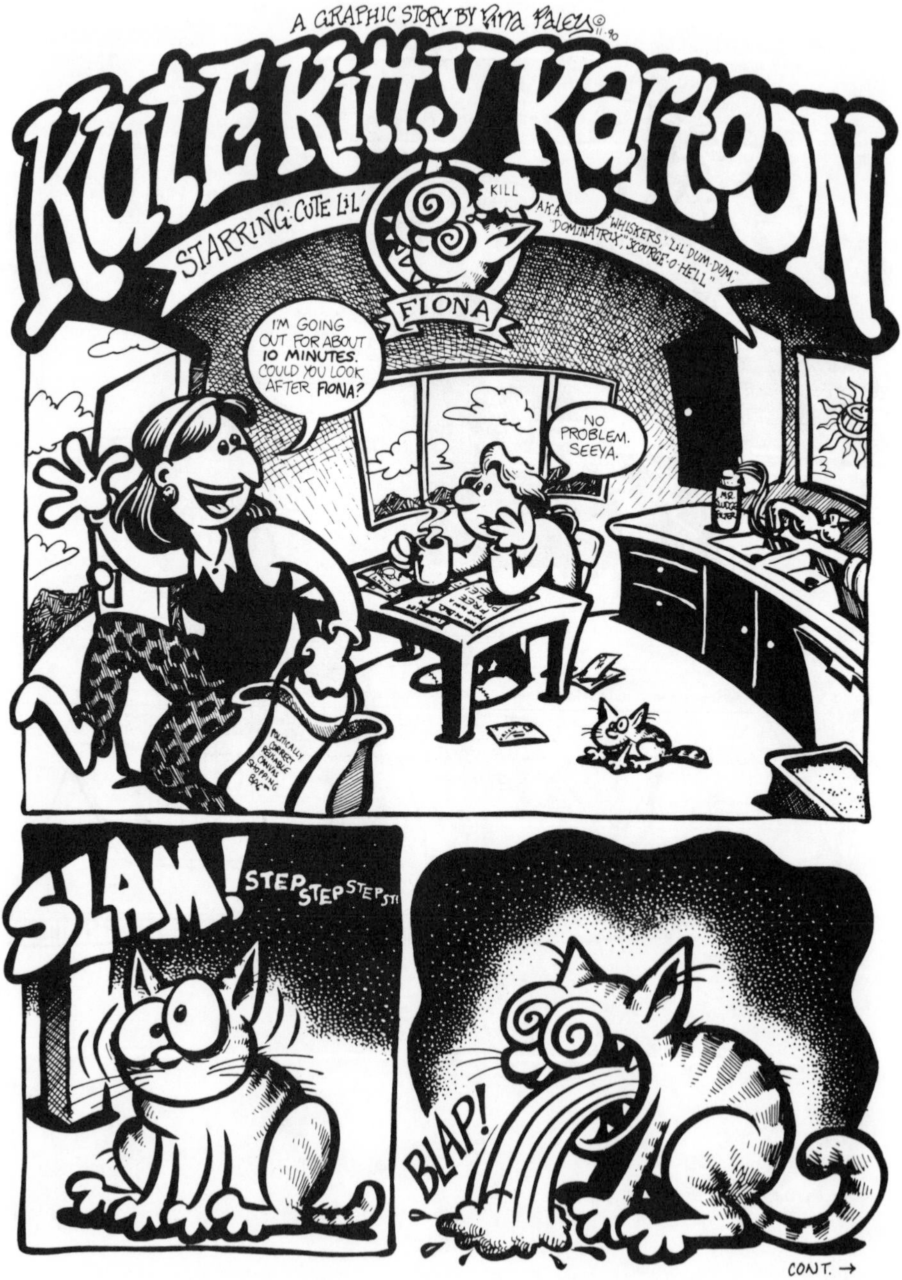
A GRAPHIC STORY BY Nina Paley © 11·90
KUTE KITTY KARTOON
STARRING: CUTE LI'L' FIONA
KILL
A.K.A. "WHISKERS," "LI'L' DUM-DUM," "DOMINATRIX," "SCOURGE-O-HELL"
I'M GOING OUT FOR ABOUT 10 MINUTES. COULD YOU LOOK AFTER FIONA?
NO PROBLEM. SEEYA.
POLITICALLY CORRECT REUSABLE CANVAS SHOPPING BAG™
SLAM!
STEP STEP STEP
BLAP!
CONT. →

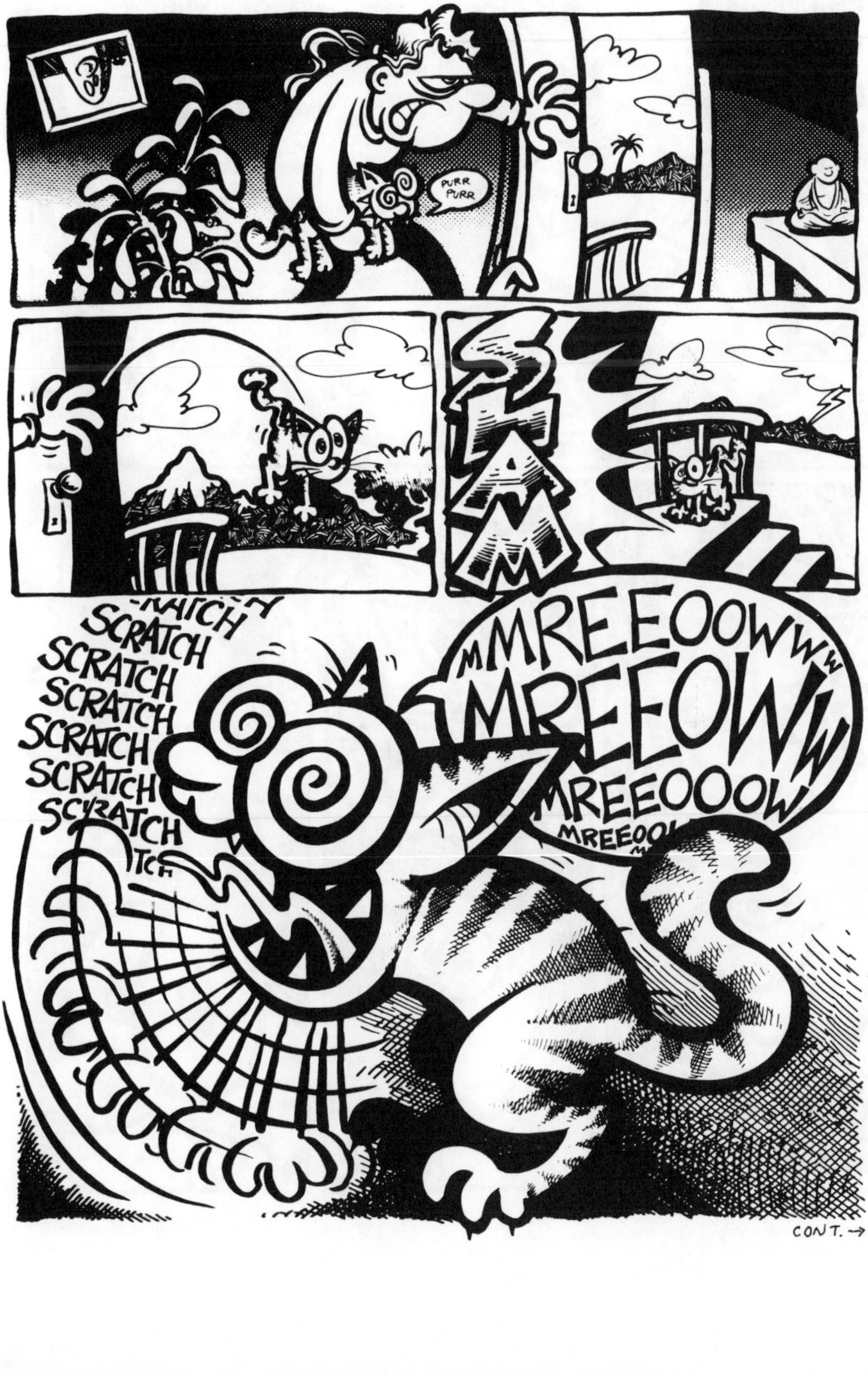
PURR PURR
SLAM
SCRATCH
SCRATCH
SCRATCH
SCRATCH
SCRATCH
MMREEOOWWW
MREEOWW
MREEOOOW

CONT. →

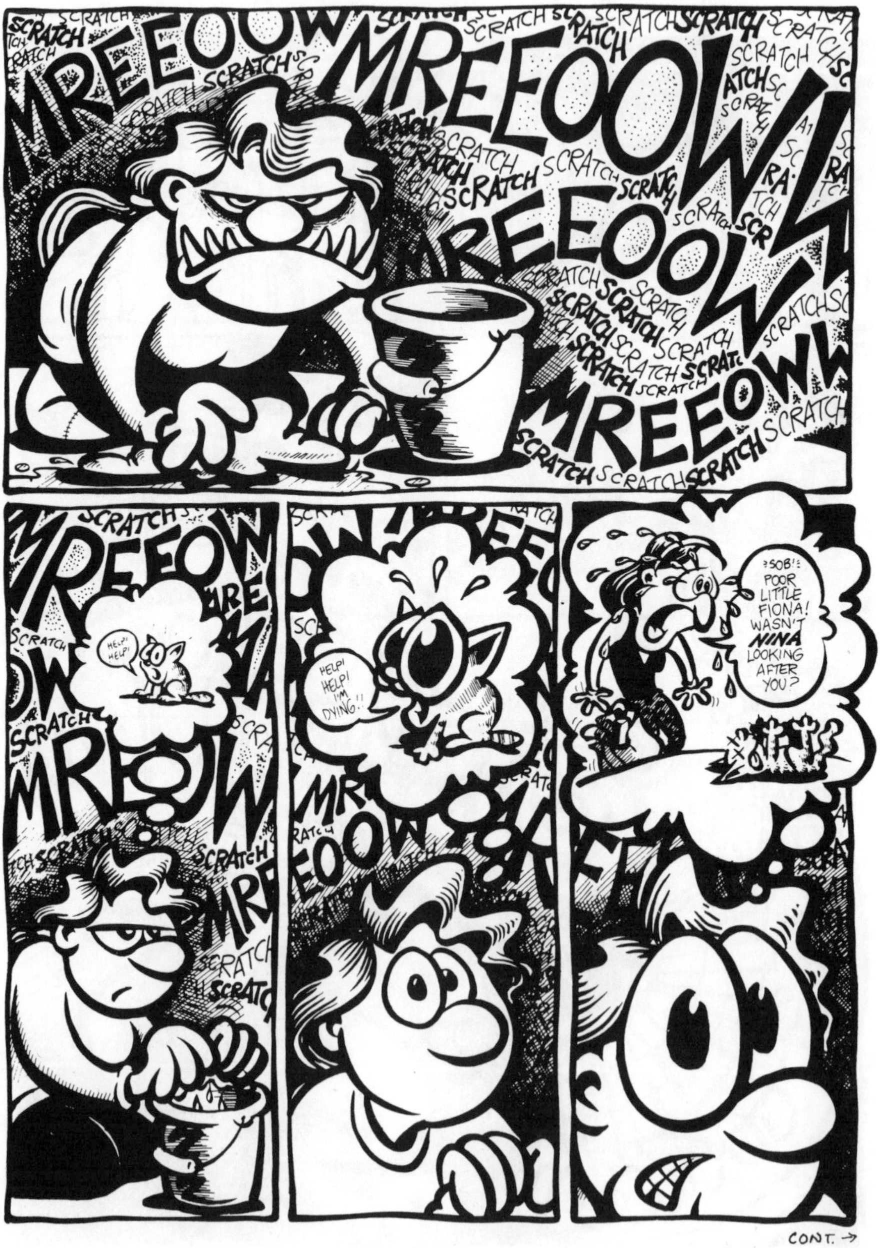
MREEOOW
SCRATCH
HELP! HELP!
HELP! HELP! I'M DYING!!
SOB! POOR LITTLE FIONA! WASN'T NINA LOOKING AFTER YOU?

CONT. →

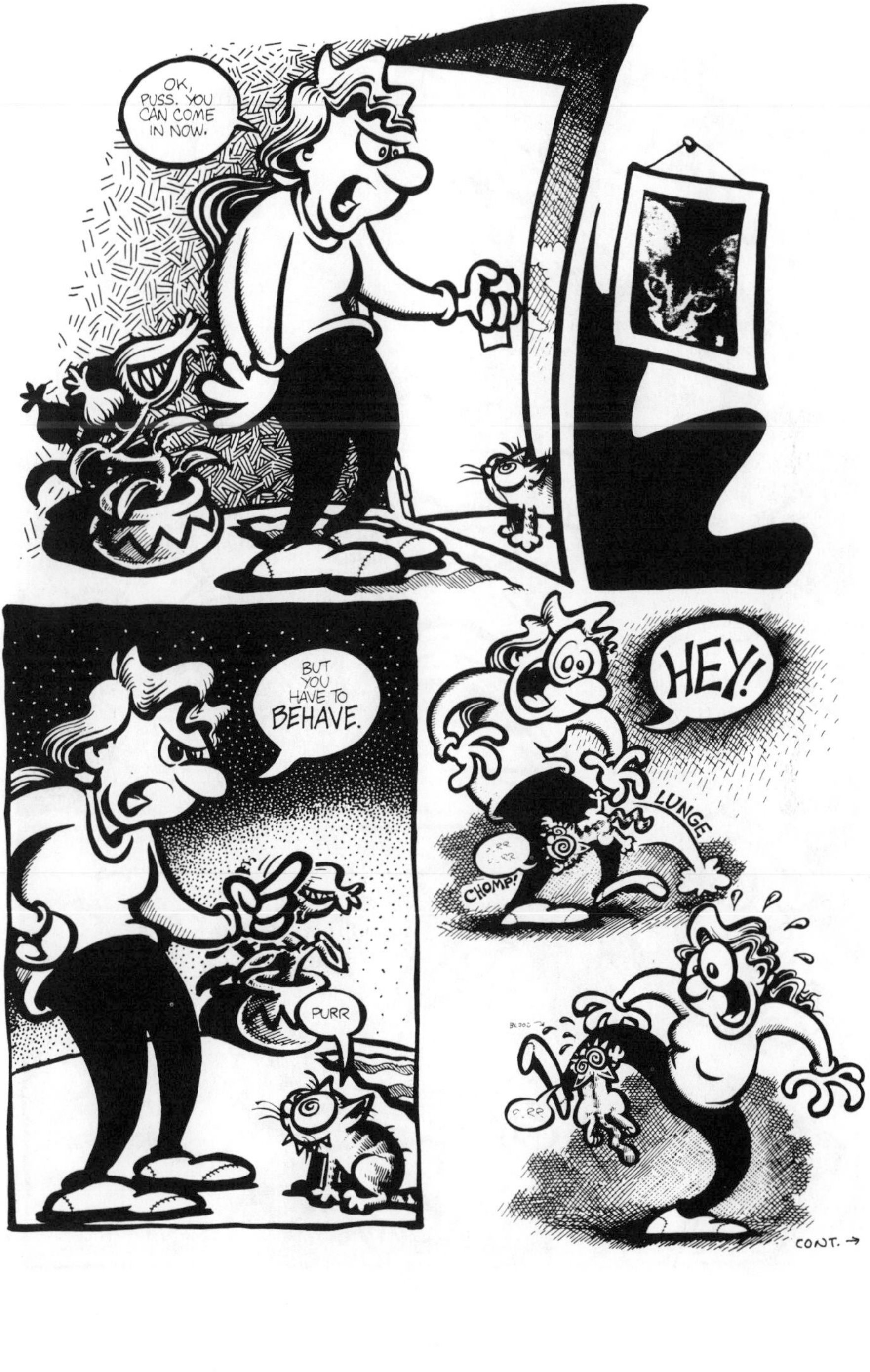
OK, PUSS. YOU CAN COME IN NOW.
BUT YOU HAVE TO BEHAVE.
PURR
HEY!
LUNGE
CHOMP!
CONT. →

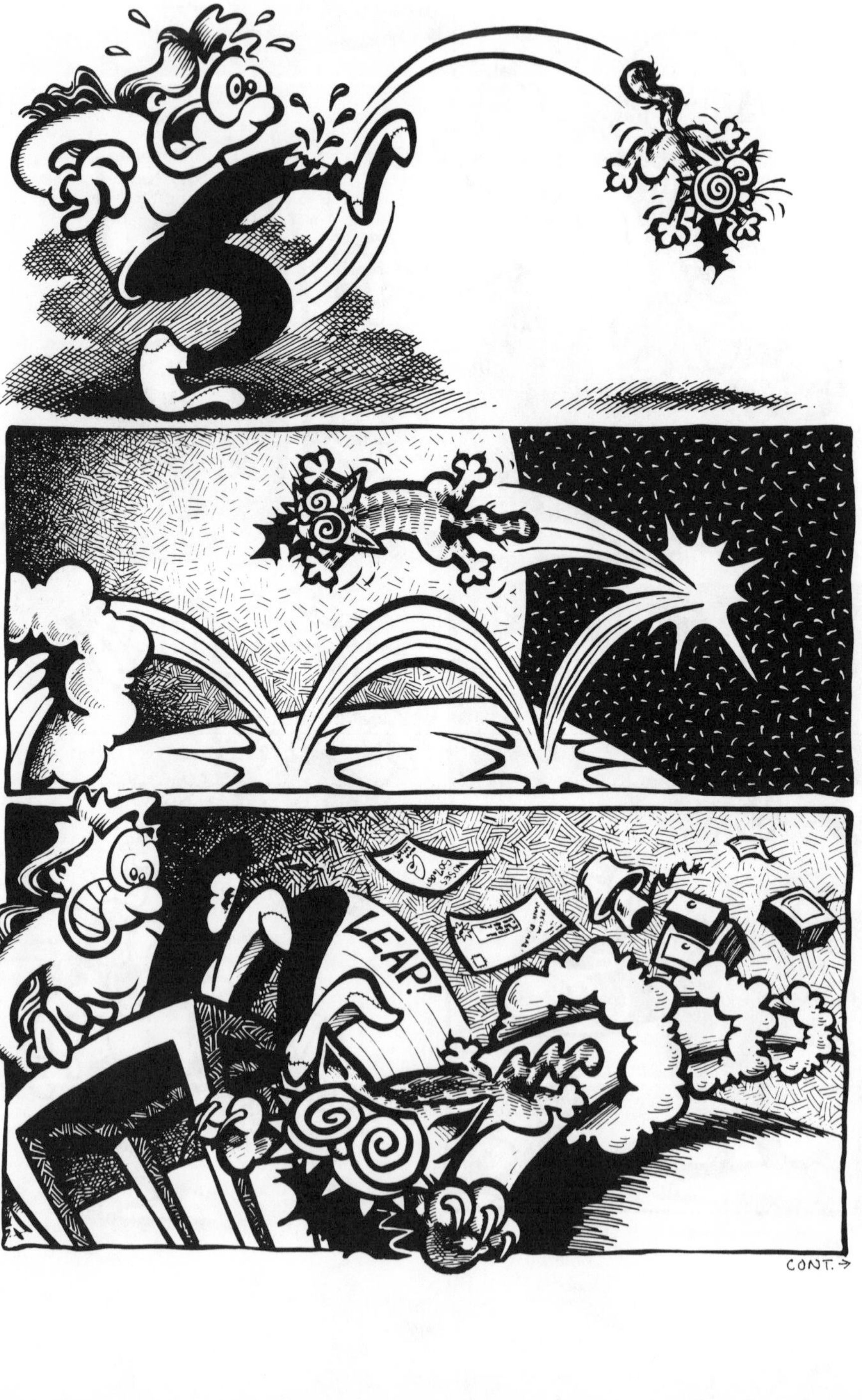
LEAP!

CONT. →

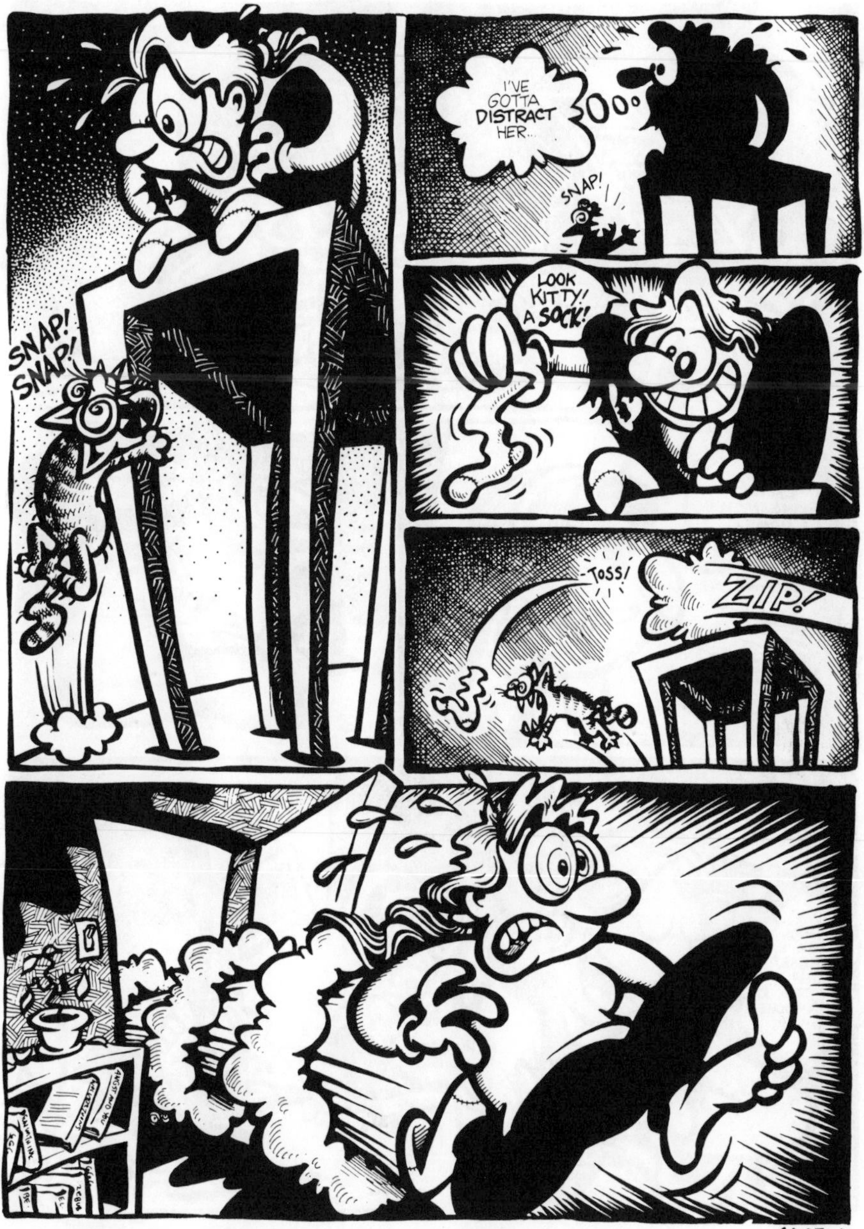
SNAP! SNAP!
I'VE GOTTA DISTRACT HER...
SNAP!
LOOK KITTY! A SOCK!
TOSS!
ZIP!

CONT. →

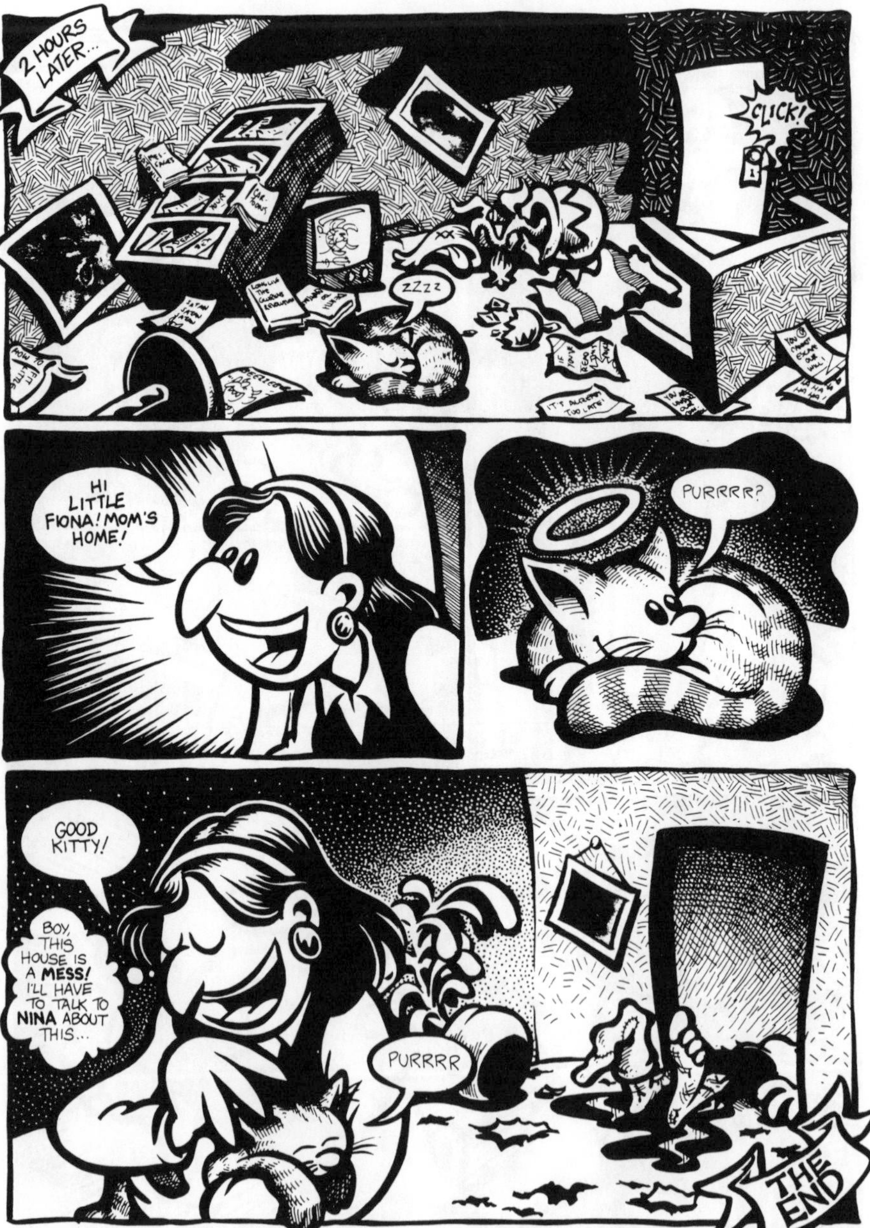
2 HOURS LATER...
CLICK!
ZZZZ
IT'S ALREADY TOO LATE!
HI LITTLE FIONA! MOM'S HOME!
PURRRRR?
GOOD KITTY!
BOY, THIS HOUSE IS A **MESS!** I'LL HAVE TO TALK TO **NINA** ABOUT THIS...
PURRRR
THE END

Marian Henley

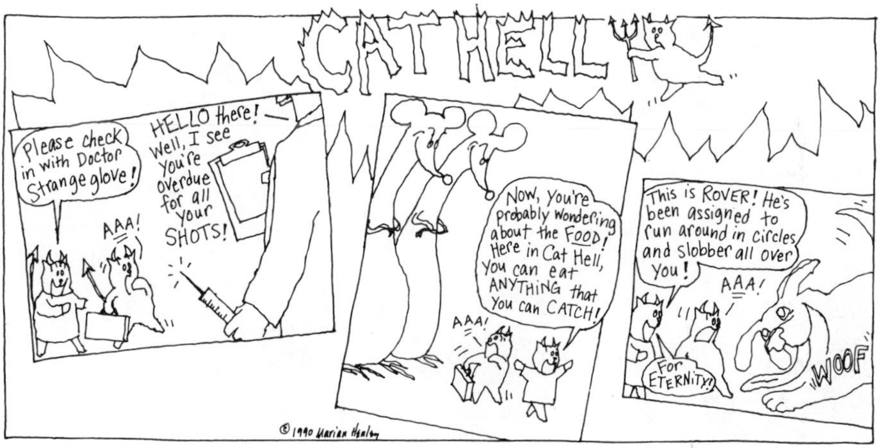
CAT HELL
Please check in with Doctor Strangeglove!
AAA!
HELLO there! Well, I see you're overdue for all your SHOTS!
Now, you're probably wondering about the FOOD! Here in Cat Hell, you can eat ANYTHING that you can CATCH!
AAA!
This is ROVER! He's been assigned to run around in circles and slobber all over you!
AAA!
For ETERNITY!
WOOF
© 1990 Marian Henley

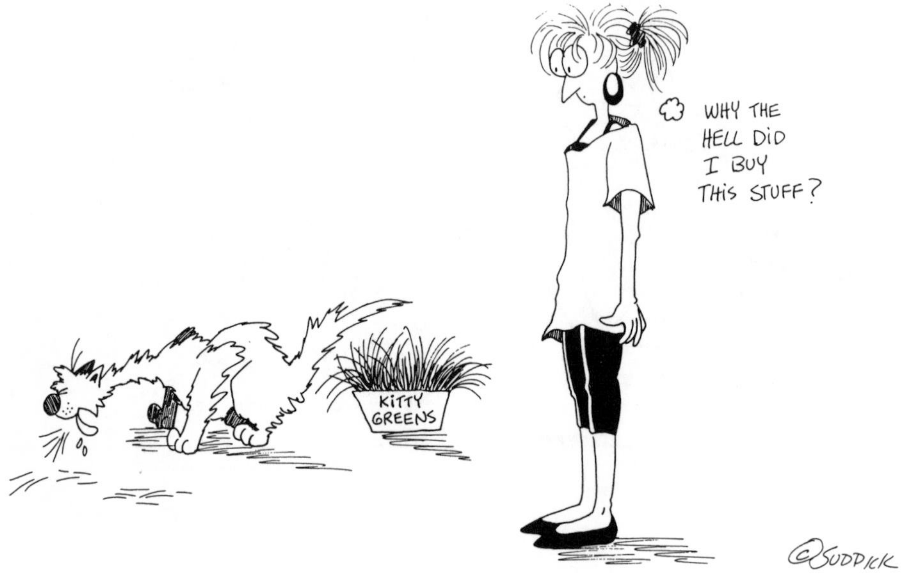
WHY THE HELL DID I BUY THIS STUFF?
KITTY GREENS
©SUDDICK

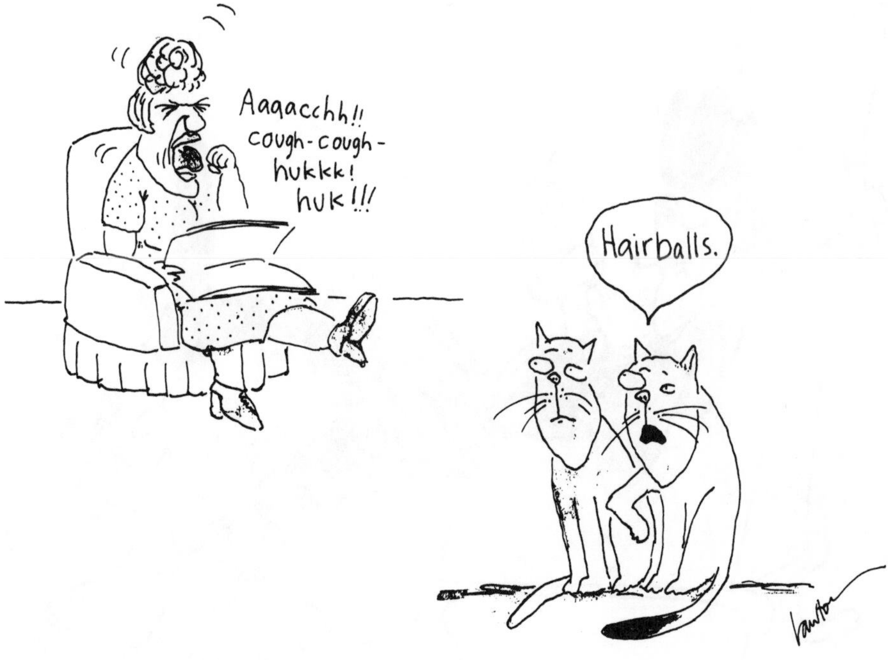
Aaqacchh!!
cough-cough-
hukkk!
huk!!!
Hairballs.
Lawton

Theresa McCracken

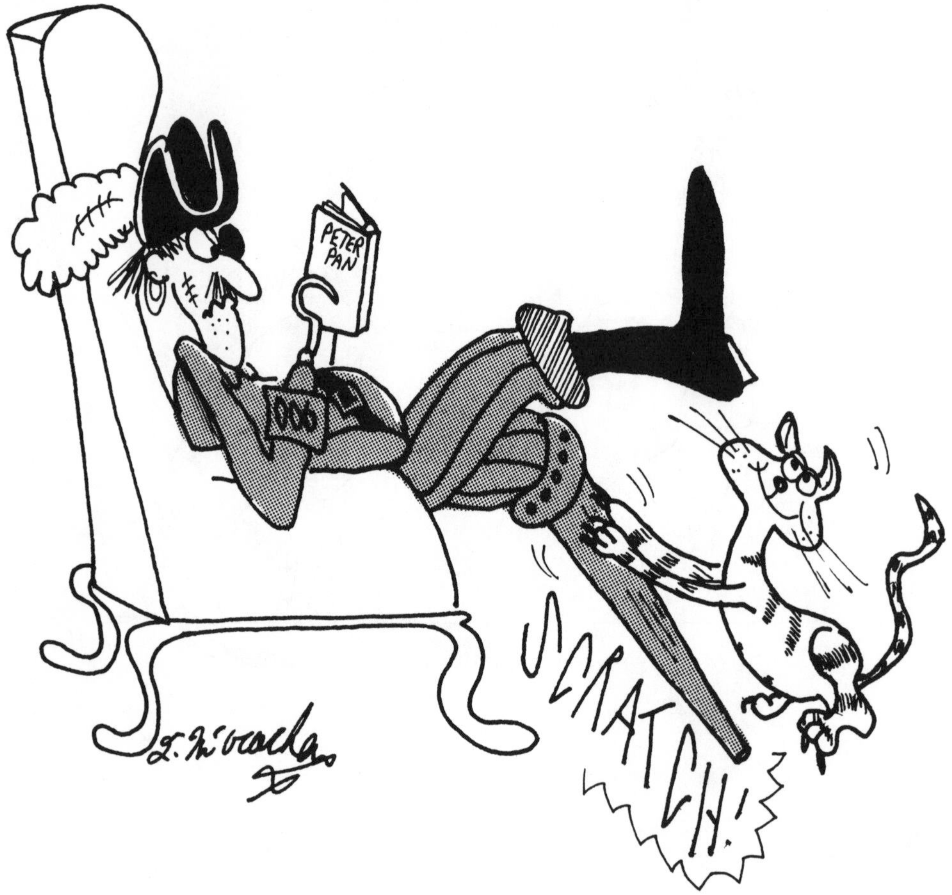
PETER PAN
SCRATCH!

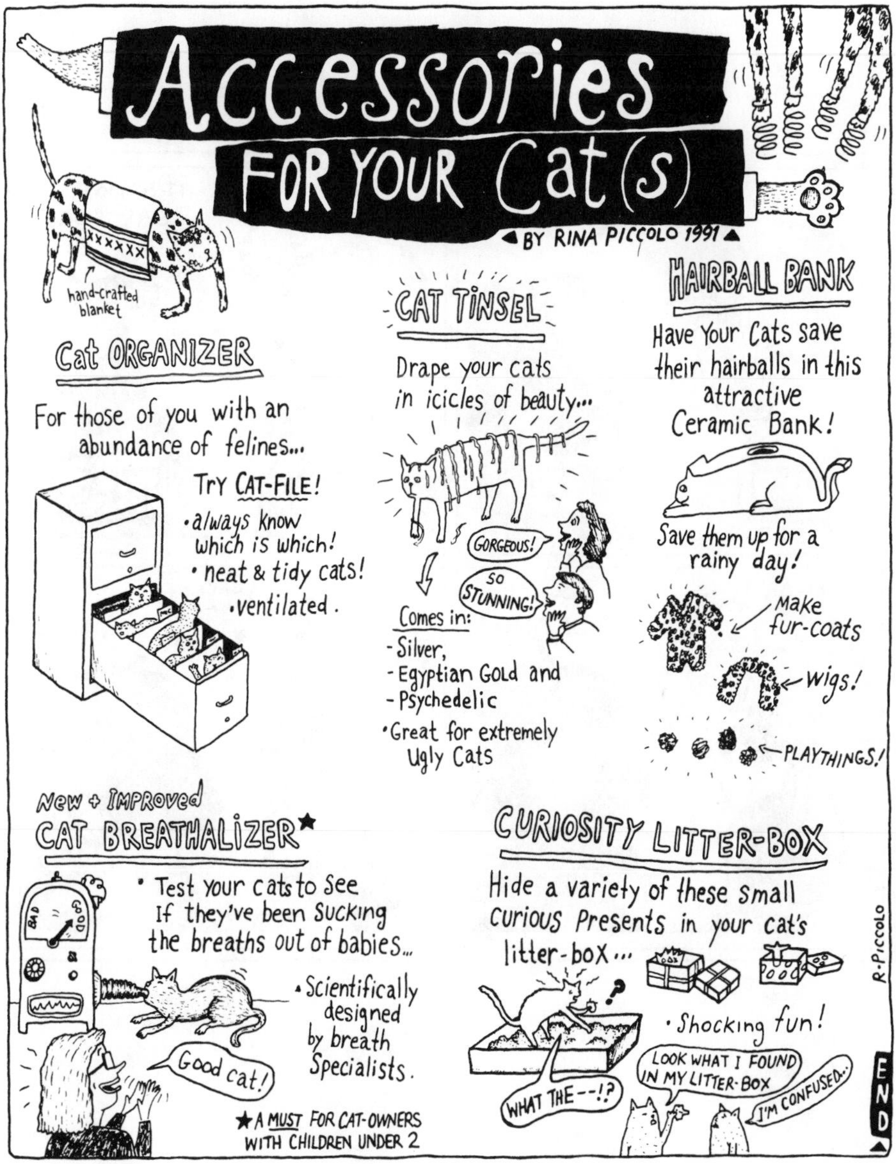
Accessories FOR YOUR Cat(s)
BY RINA PICCOLO 1991
hand-crafted blanket
Cat ORGANIZER
For those of you with an abundance of felines...
Try CAT-FILE!
•always know which is which!
•neat & tidy cats!
•ventilated.
CAT TINSEL
Drape your cats in icicles of beauty...
GORGEOUS!
SO STUNNING!
Comes in:
- Silver,
- Egyptian Gold and
- Psychedelic
•Great for extremely Ugly Cats
HAIRBALL BANK
Have Your Cats save their hairballs in this attractive Ceramic Bank!
Save them up for a rainy day!
Make fur-coats
wigs!
PLAYTHINGS!
New + Improved
CAT BREATHALIZER★
BAD
GOOD
• Test your cats to see If they've been sucking the breaths out of babies...
• Scientifically designed by breath Specialists.
Good cat!
★A MUST FOR CAT-OWNERS WITH CHILDREN UNDER 2
CURIOSITY LITTER-BOX
Hide a variety of these small curious Presents in your cat's litter-box...
• Shocking fun!
WHAT THE--!?
LOOK WHAT I FOUND IN MY LITTER-BOX
I'M CONFUSED...
R-PICCOLO
END

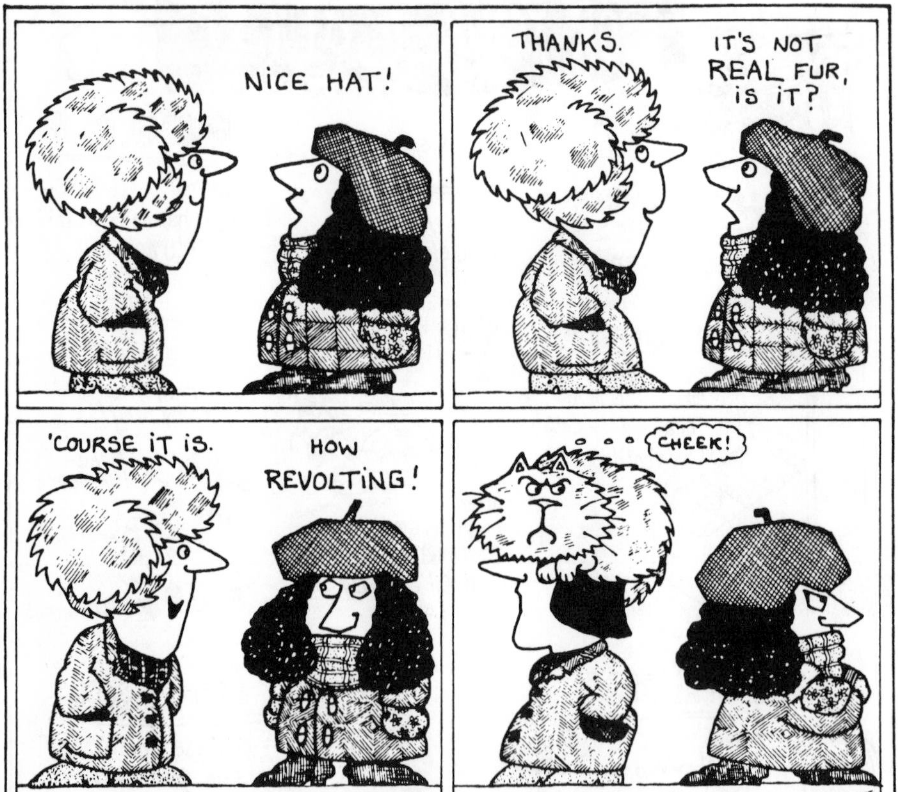
NICE HAT!
THANKS.
IT'S NOT REAL FUR, IS IT?
'COURSE IT IS.
HOW REVOLTING!
CHEEK!

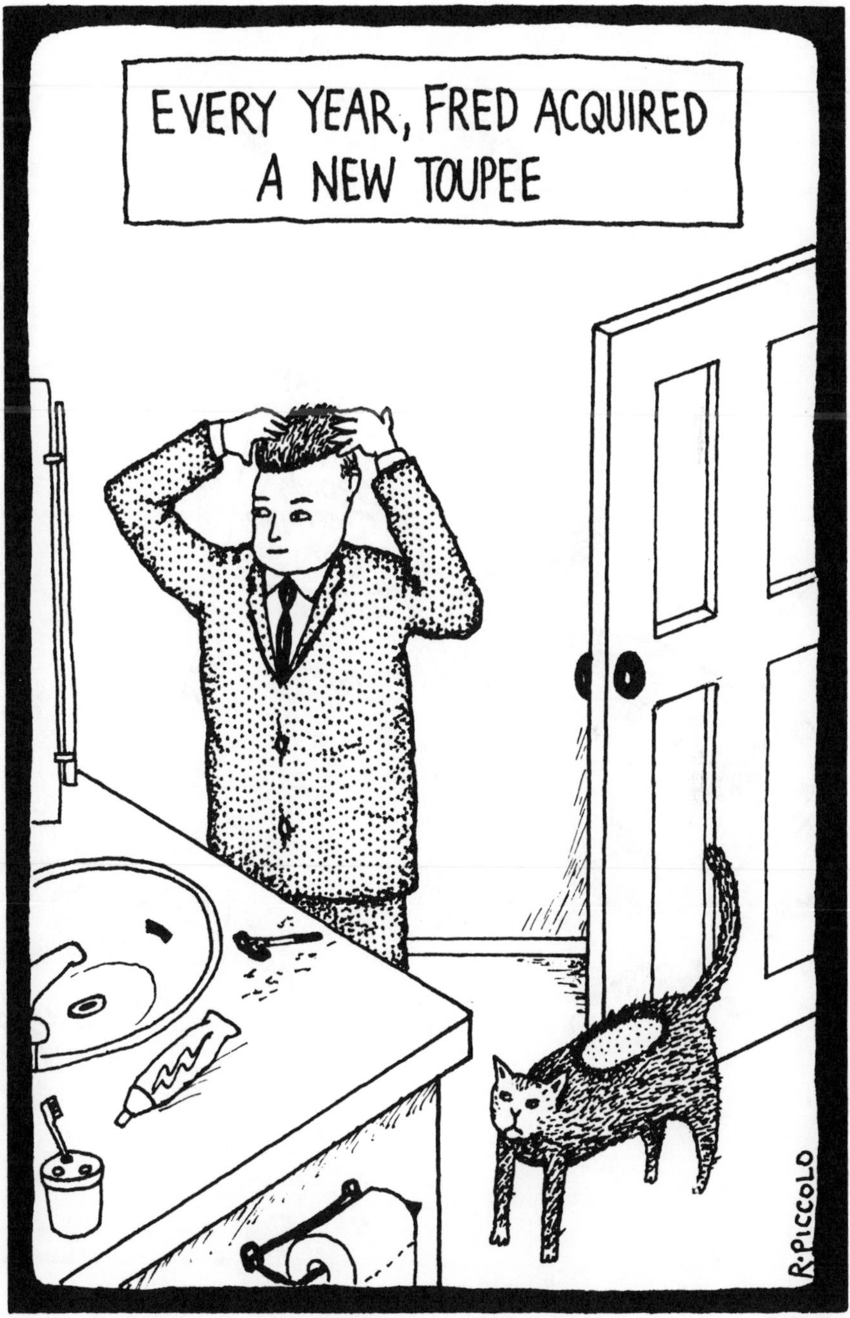
EVERY YEAR, FRED ACQUIRED A NEW TOUPEE
R. PICCOLO

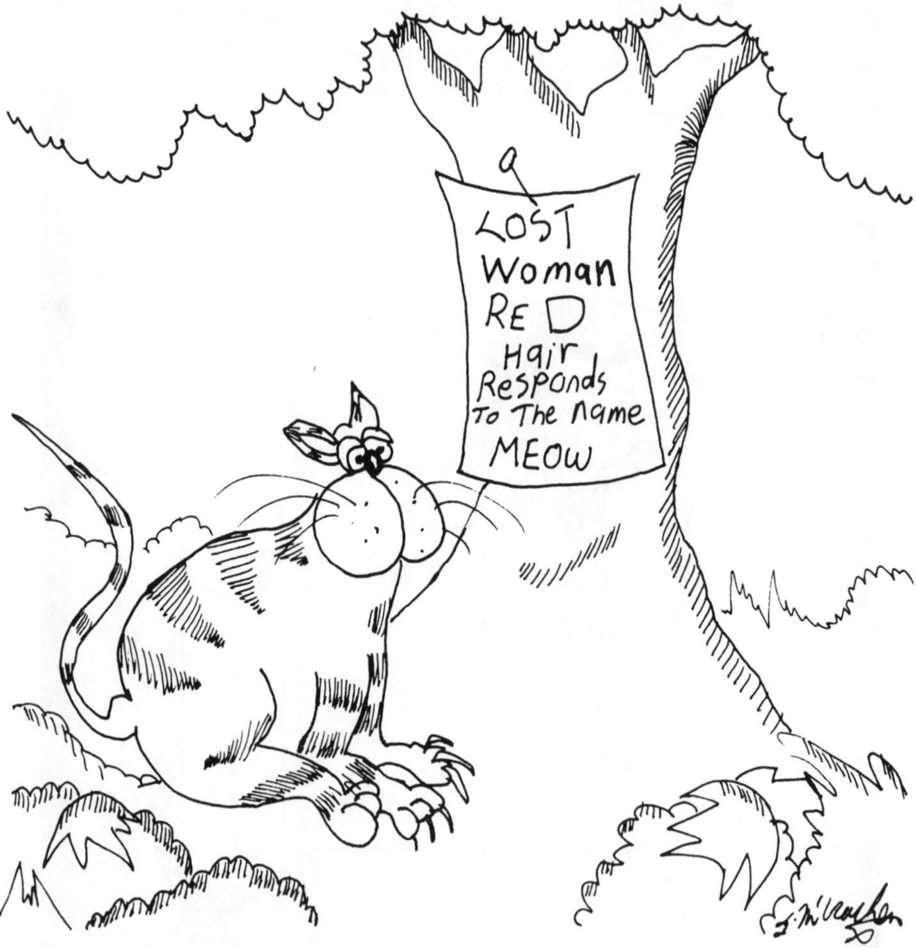
a
LOST
Woman
RED
Hair
Responds
To The name
MEOW

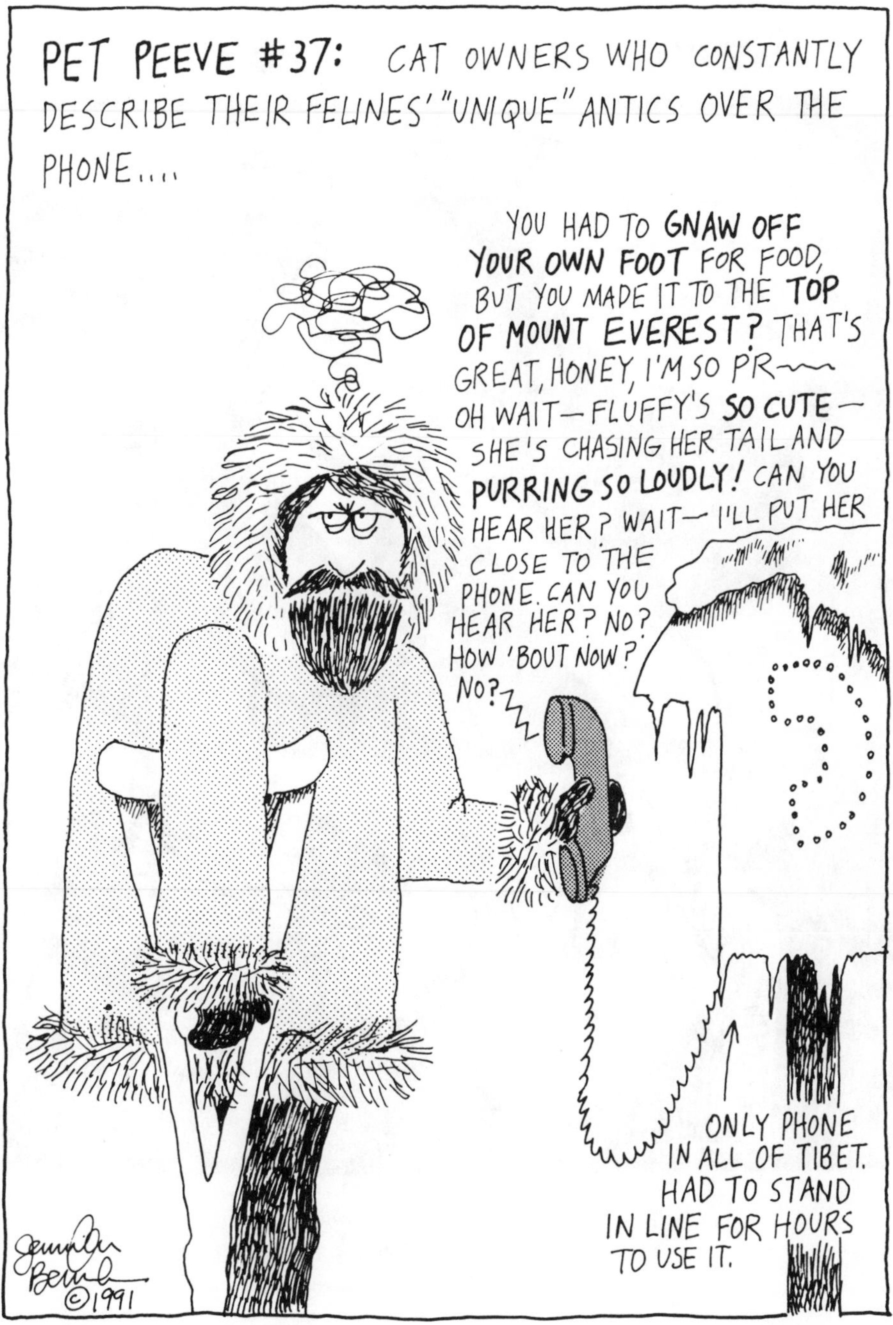
PET PEEVE #37: CAT OWNERS WHO CONSTANTLY DESCRIBE THEIR FELINES' "UNIQUE" ANTICS OVER THE PHONE....
YOU HAD TO GNAW OFF YOUR OWN FOOT FOR FOOD, BUT YOU MADE IT TO THE TOP OF MOUNT EVEREST? THAT'S GREAT, HONEY, I'M SO PR— OH WAIT— FLUFFY'S SO CUTE— SHE'S CHASING HER TAIL AND PURRING SO LOUDLY! CAN YOU HEAR HER? WAIT— I'LL PUT HER CLOSE TO THE PHONE. CAN YOU HEAR HER? NO? HOW 'BOUT NOW? NO?
ONLY PHONE IN ALL OF TIBET. HAD TO STAND IN LINE FOR HOURS TO USE IT.
Jennifer Berman ©1991

STONEWALL RIOTS

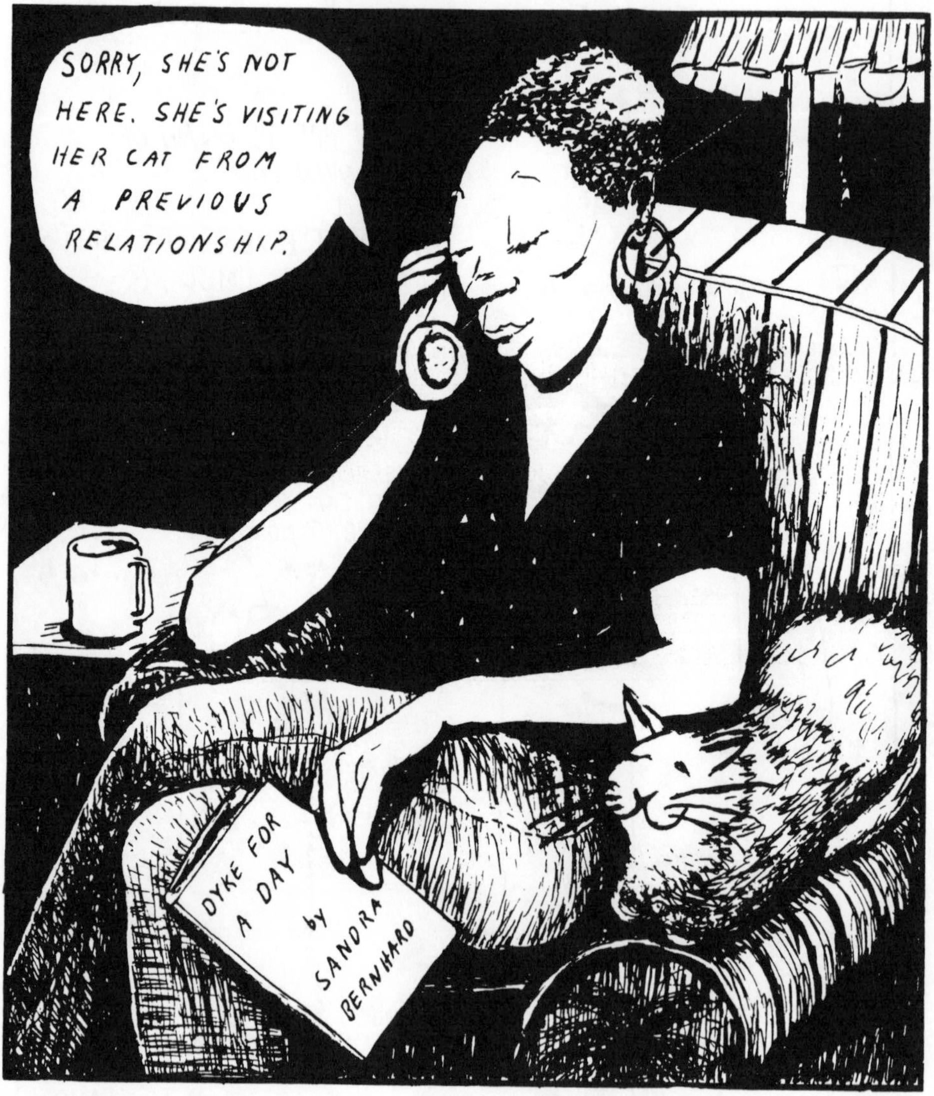
SORRY, SHE'S NOT HERE. SHE'S VISITING HER CAT FROM A PREVIOUS RELATIONSHIP.
DYKE FOR A DAY by SANDRA BERNHARD

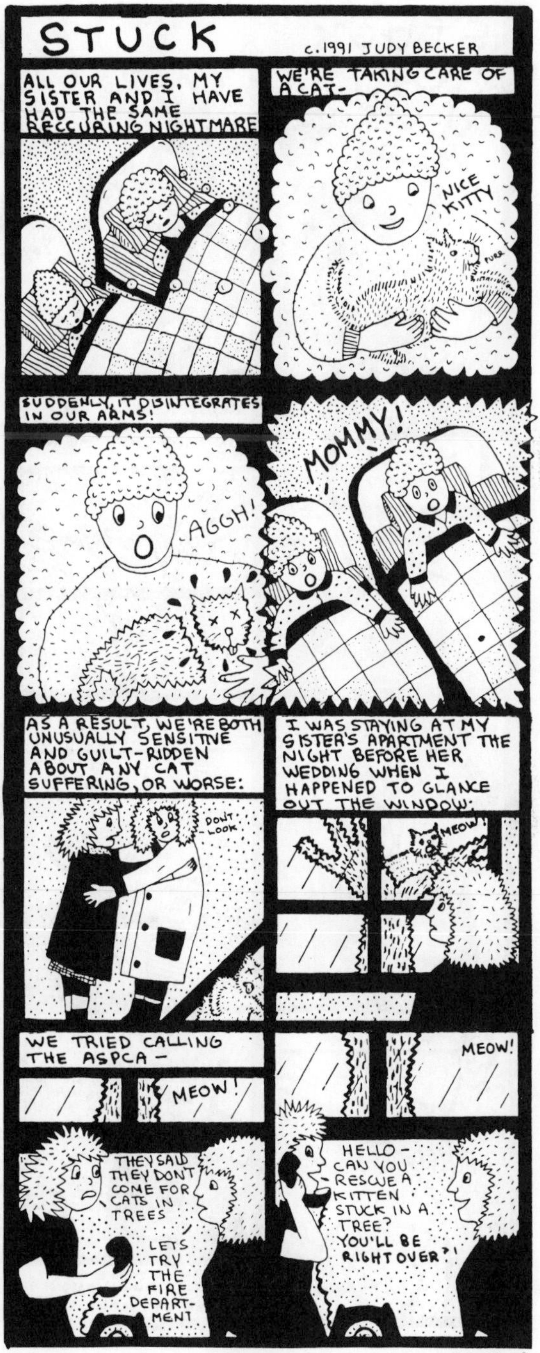
STUCK
c.1991 JUDY BECKER
ALL OUR LIVES, MY SISTER AND I HAVE HAD THE SAME RECCURING NIGHTMARE
WE'RE TAKING CARE OF A CAT-
NICE KITTY
PURR
SUDDENLY, IT DISINTEGRATES IN OUR ARMS!
AGGH!
MOMMY!
AS A RESULT, WE'RE BOTH UNUSUALLY SENSITIVE AND GUILT-RIDDEN ABOUT ANY CAT SUFFERING, OR WORSE:
DON'T LOOK
I WAS STAYING AT MY SISTER'S APARTMENT THE NIGHT BEFORE HER WEDDING WHEN I HAPPENED TO GLANCE OUT THE WINDOW:
MEOW!
WE TRIED CALLING THE ASPCA -
MEOW!
THEY SAID THEY DON'T COME FOR CATS IN TREES
LETS TRY THE FIRE DEPARTMENT
MEOW!
HELLO - CAN YOU RESCUE A KITTEN STUCK IN A TREE? YOU'LL BE RIGHT OVER?!

CONT. →

Judy Becker

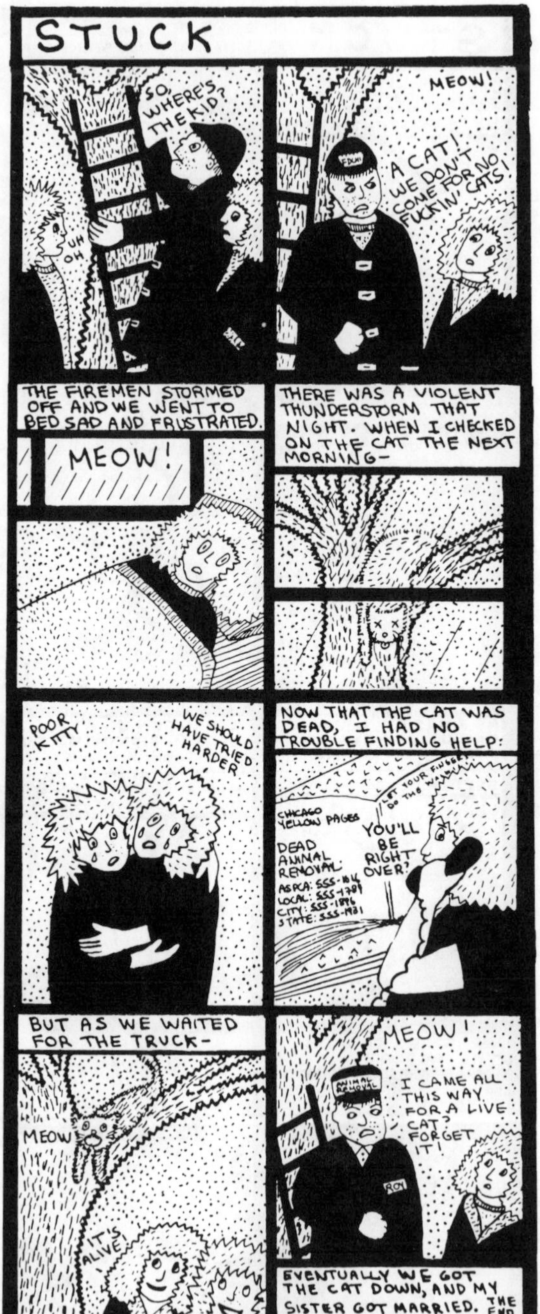
STUCK
SO, WHERE'S THE KID?
UH OH
MEOW!
A CAT! WE DON'T COME FOR NO FUCKIN' CATS!
THE FIREMEN STORMED OFF AND WE WENT TO BED SAD AND FRUSTRATED.
MEOW!
THERE WAS A VIOLENT THUNDERSTORM THAT NIGHT. WHEN I CHECKED ON THE CAT THE NEXT MORNING–
POOR KITTY
WE SHOULD HAVE TRIED HARDER
NOW THAT THE CAT WAS DEAD, I HAD NO TROUBLE FINDING HELP:
CHICAGO YELLOW PAGES
DEAD ANIMAL REMOVAL:
YOU'LL BE RIGHT OVER?
BUT AS WE WAITED FOR THE TRUCK–
MEOW
IT'S ALIVE!
MEOW!
I CAME ALL THIS WAY FOR A LIVE CAT? FORGET IT!
ROY
EVENTUALLY WE GOT THE CAT DOWN, AND MY SISTER GOT MARRIED. THE END

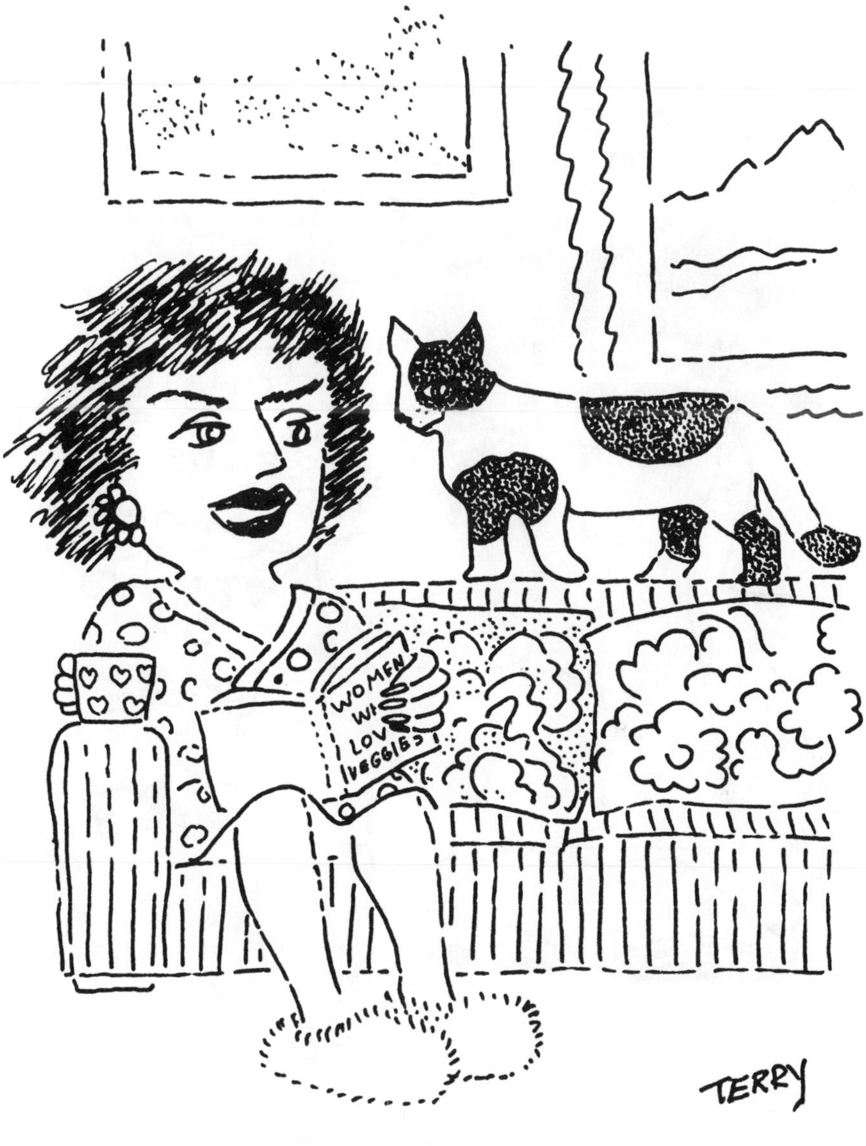
WOMEN WI LOVE VEGGIES
TERRY

Men are like cats. The only time you find them between your legs is when they want something.

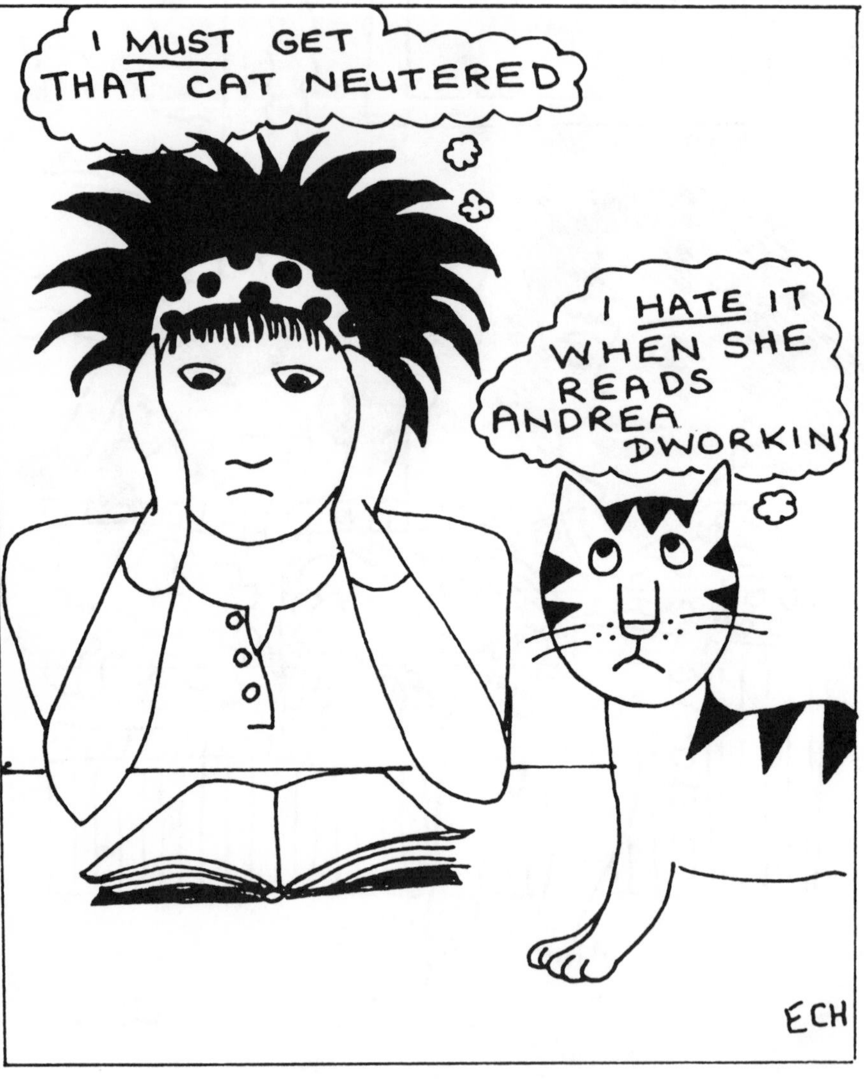
I MUST GET THAT CAT NEUTERED
I HATE IT WHEN SHE READS ANDREA DWORKIN
ECH

Posy Simmonds

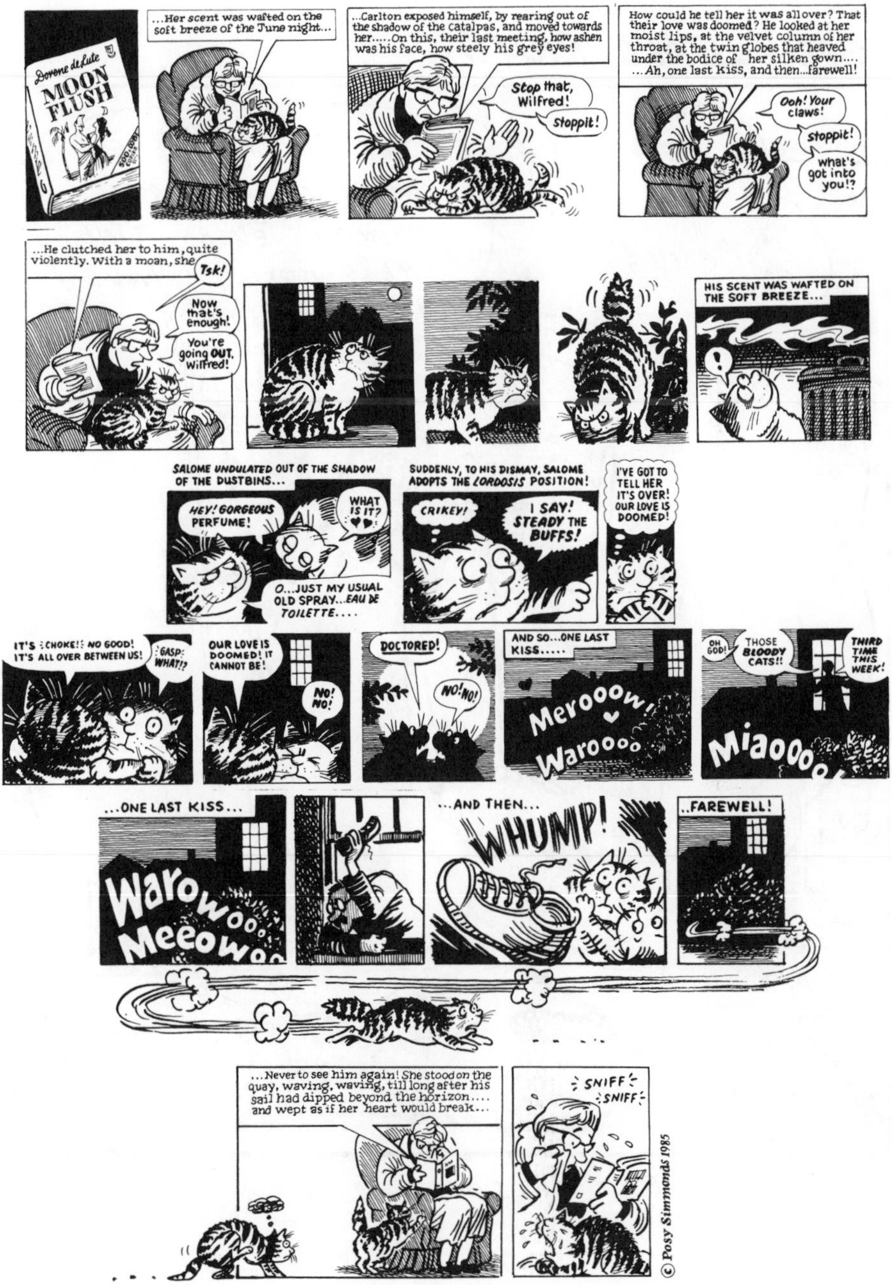

Dorene de Lute
MOON FLUSH
...Her scent was wafted on the soft breeze of the June night...
...Carlton exposed himself, by rearing out of the shadow of the catalpas, and moved towards her.....On this, their last meeting, how ashen was his face, how steely his grey eyes!
Stop that, Wilfred!
Stoppit!
How could he tell her it was all over? That their love was doomed? He looked at her moist lips, at the velvet column of her throat, at the twin globes that heaved under the bodice of her silken gown.... ...Ah, one last kiss, and then...farewell!
Ooh! Your claws!
Stoppit!
what's got into you!?
...He clutched her to him, quite violently. With a moan, she
Tsk!
Now that's enough!
You're going OUT, Wilfred!
HIS SCENT WAS WAFTED ON THE SOFT BREEZE...
!
SALOME UNDULATED OUT OF THE SHADOW OF THE DUSTBINS...
HEY! GORGEOUS PERFUME!
WHAT IS IT?
O...JUST MY USUAL OLD SPRAY...EAU DE TOILETTE....
SUDDENLY, TO HIS DISMAY, SALOME ADOPTS THE LORDOSIS POSITION!
CRIKEY!
I SAY! STEADY THE BUFFS!
I'VE GOT TO TELL HER IT'S OVER! OUR LOVE IS DOOMED!
IT'S CHOKE! NO GOOD! IT'S ALL OVER BETWEEN US!
GASP: WHAT!?
OUR LOVE IS DOOMED! IT CANNOT BE!
NO! NO!
DOCTORED!
NO! NO!
AND SO...ONE LAST KISS.....
Merooow!
Waroooo
OH GOD!
THOSE BLOODY CATS!!
THIRD TIME THIS WEEK!
Miaoooo!
...ONE LAST KISS...
Warowooo
Meeowo
...AND THEN...
WHUMP!
..FAREWELL!
...Never to see him again! She stood on the quay, waving, waving, till long after his sail had dipped beyond the horizon.... and wept as if her heart would break...
SNIFF
SNIFF
© Posy Simmonds 1985

STONEWALL RIOTS

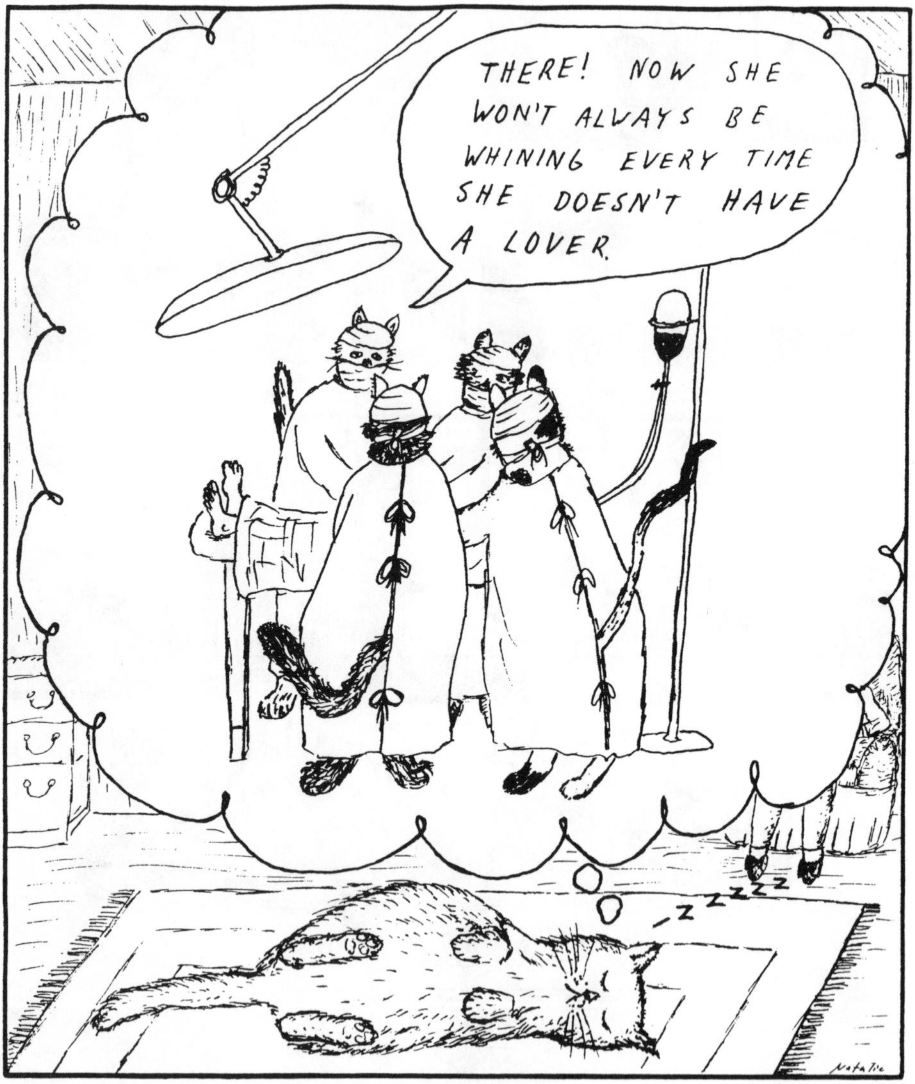
THERE! NOW SHE WON'T ALWAYS BE WHINING EVERY TIME SHE DOESN'T HAVE A LOVER.
Z Z Z Z Z Z
Natalie

TABBY DREAMS SHE TAKES LOUISE TO GET FIXED.

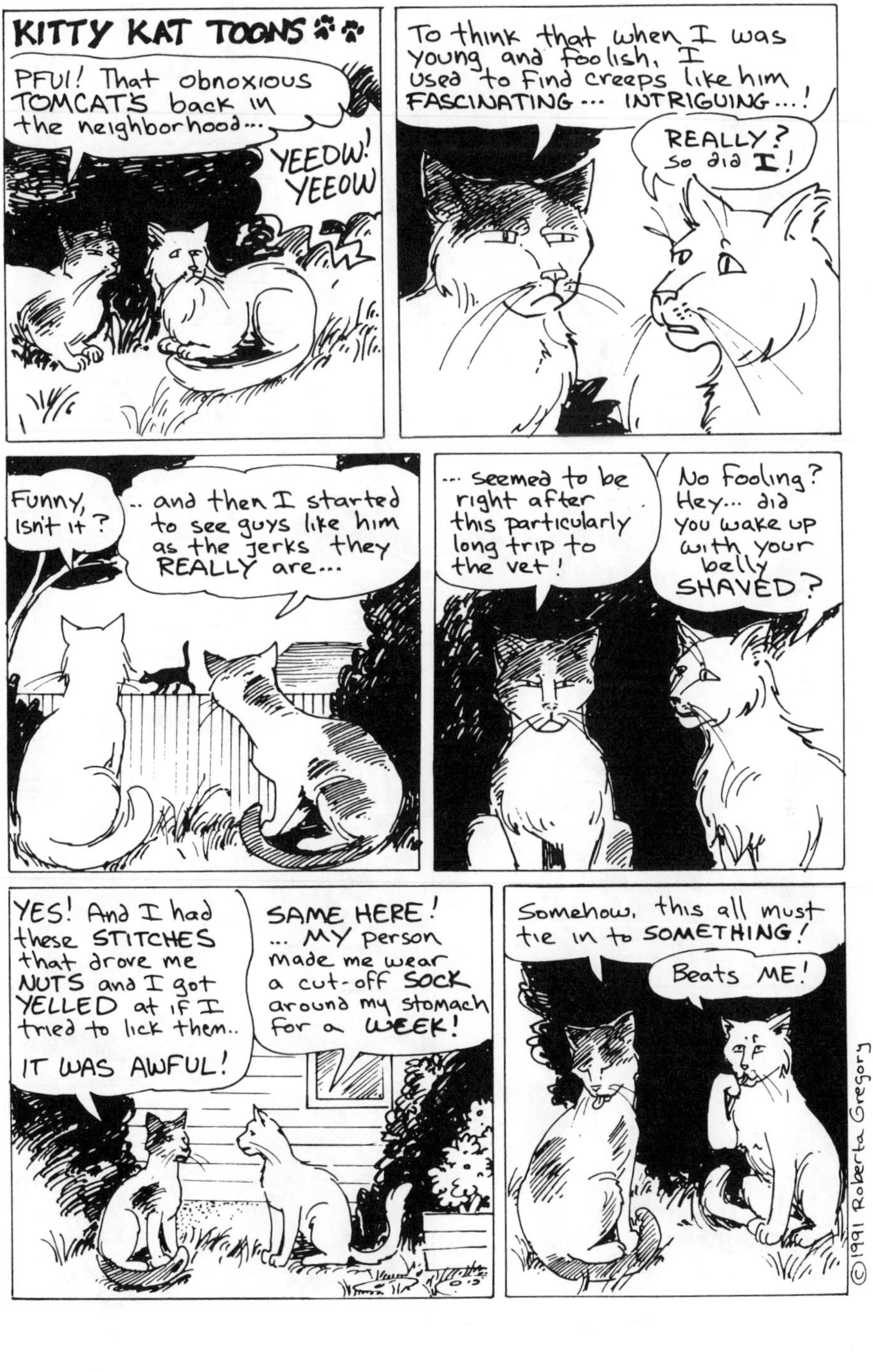
KITTY KAT TOONS
PFUI! That obnoxious TOMCAT'S back in the neighborhood...
YEEOW! YEEOW
To think that when I was young and foolish, I used to find creeps like him FASCINATING... INTRIGUING...!
REALLY? so did I!
Funny, isn't it?
.. and then I started to see guys like him as the jerks they REALLY are...
... seemed to be right after this particularly long trip to the vet!
No fooling? Hey... did you wake up with your belly SHAVED?
YES! And I had these STITCHES that drove me NUTS and I got YELLED at if I tried to lick them..
IT WAS AWFUL!
SAME HERE! ... MY person made me wear a cut-off SOCK around my stomach for a WEEK!
Somehow, this all must tie in to SOMETHING!
Beats ME!
©1991 Roberta Gregory

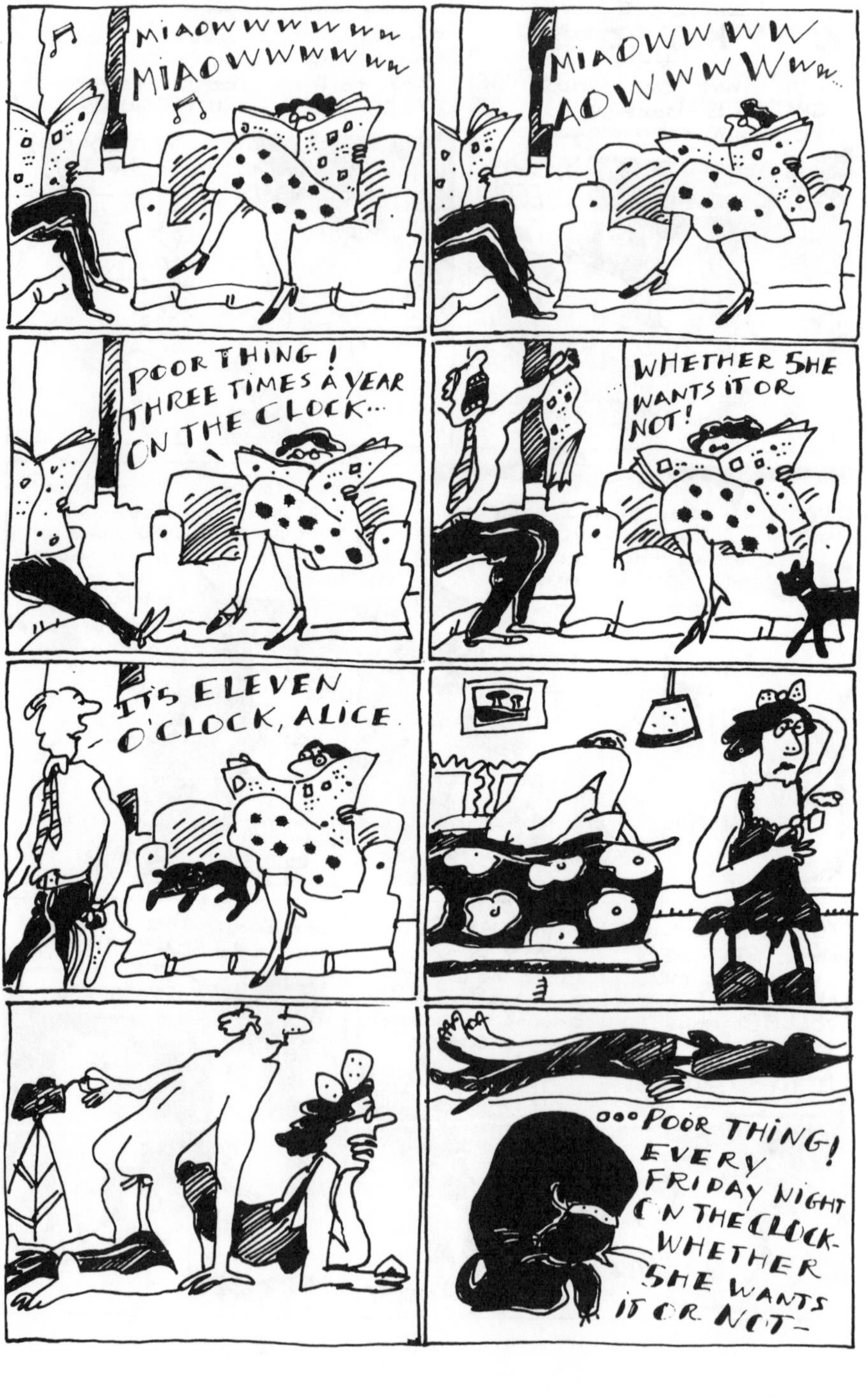
MIAOWWWWWWW
MIAOWWWWWWW
MIAOWWWWW
AOWWWWWW...
POOR THING! THREE TIMES A YEAR ON THE CLOCK...
WHETHER SHE WANTS IT OR NOT!
IT'S ELEVEN O'CLOCK, ALICE.
...POOR THING! EVERY FRIDAY NIGHT ON THE CLOCK- WHETHER SHE WANTS IT OR NOT-

SO, IS IT A MALE OR FEMALE CAT?
HE'S A FLEA MALE.
YECH!
SCRATCH
SCRATCH

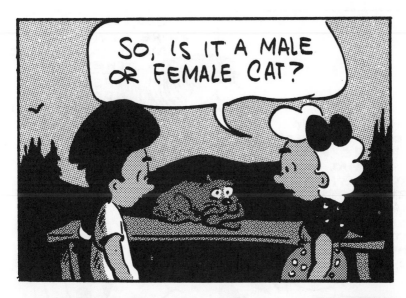

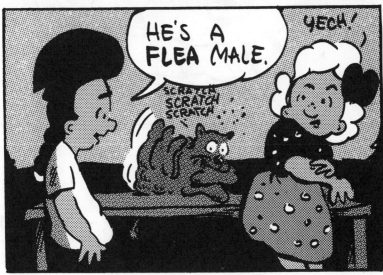

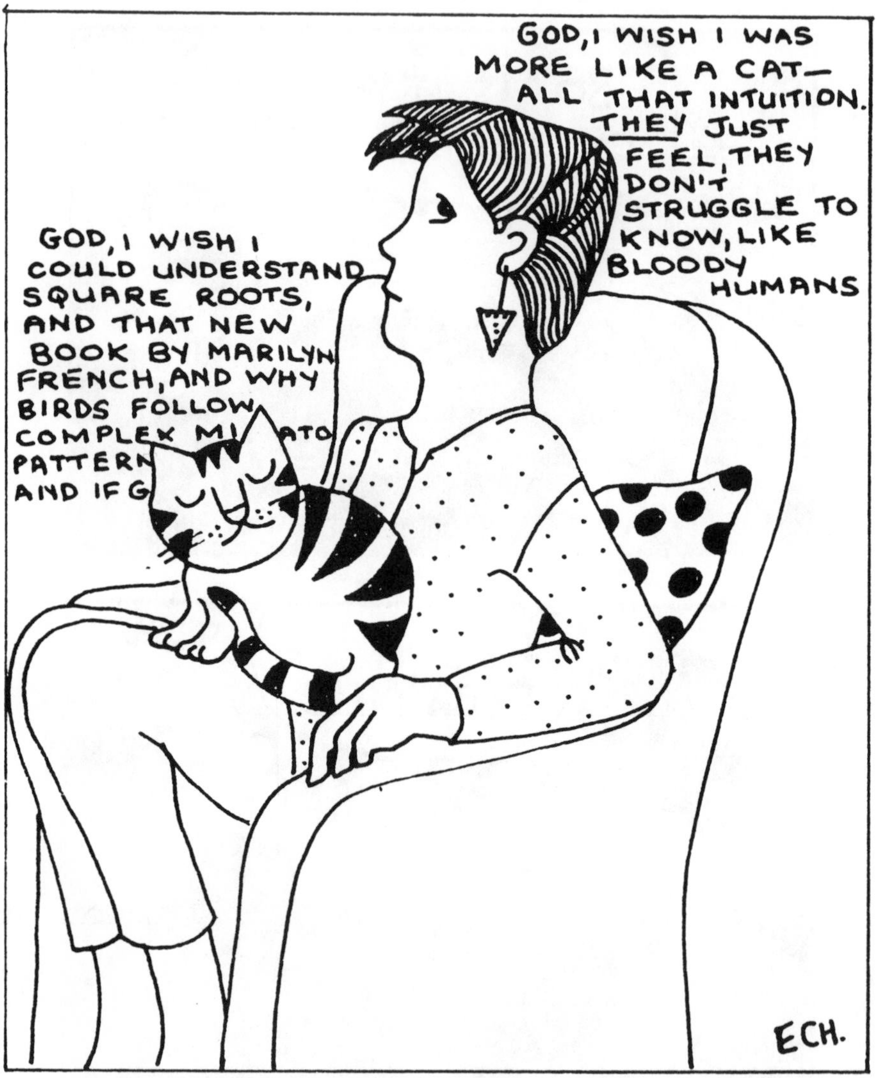
GOD, I WISH I WAS MORE LIKE A CAT— ALL THAT INTUITION. THEY JUST FEEL, THEY DON'T STRUGGLE TO KNOW, LIKE BLOODY HUMANS
GOD, I WISH I COULD UNDERSTAND SQUARE ROOTS, AND THAT NEW BOOK BY MARILYN FRENCH, AND WHY BIRDS FOLLOW COMPLEX MI ATO PATTERN AND IF G
ECH.

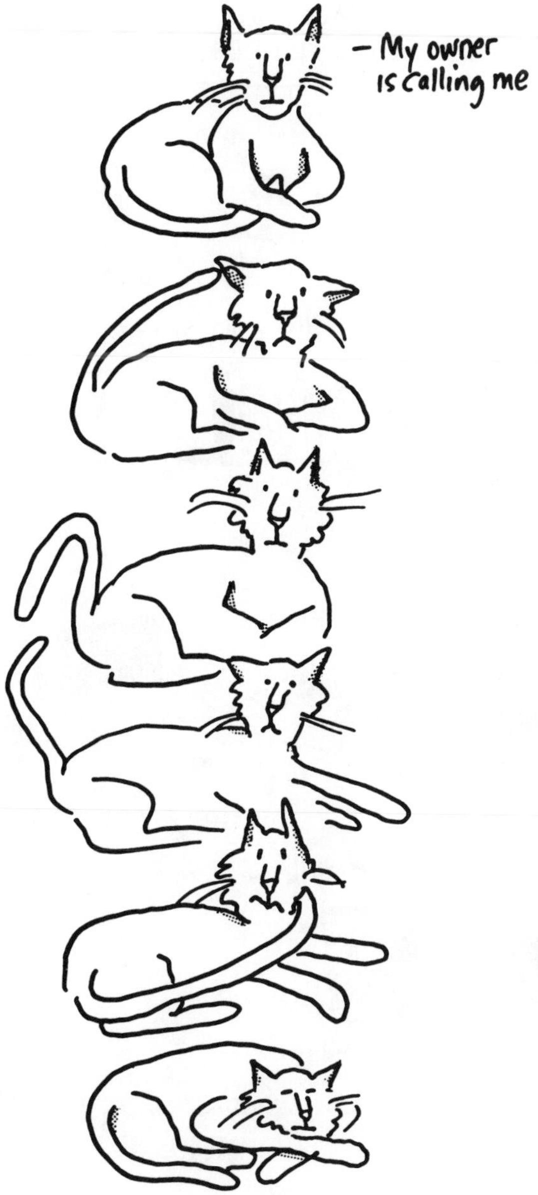
- My owner
is calling me

Roz Chast

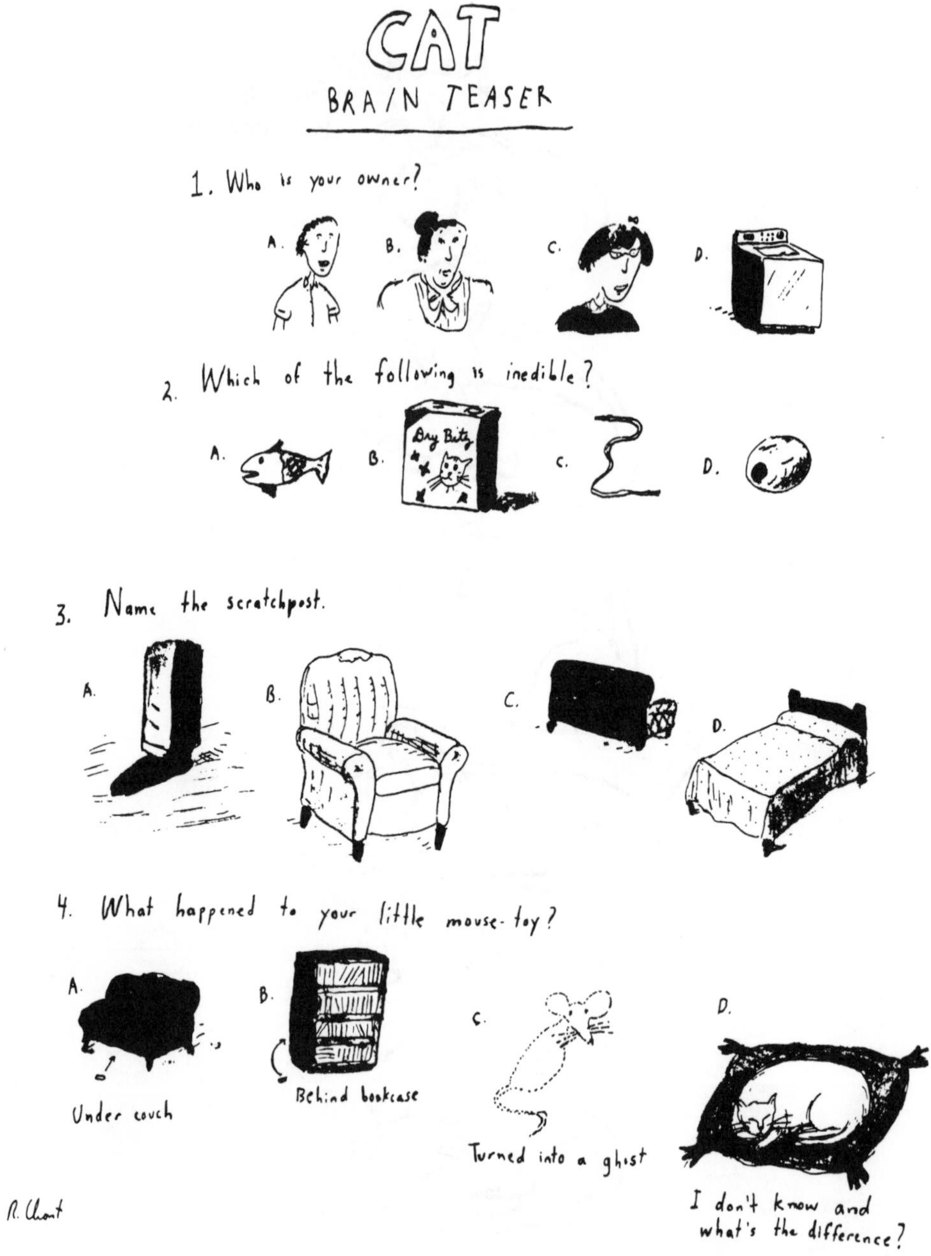
CAT
BRAIN TEASER
1. Who is your owner?
A.
B.
C.
D.
2. Which of the following is inedible?
A.
B.
Dry Bitz
C.
D.
3. Name the scratchpost.
A.
B.
C.
D.
4. What happened to your little mouse-toy?
A.
Under couch
B.
Behind bookcase
C.
Turned into a ghost
D.
I don't know and what's the difference?
R. Chast

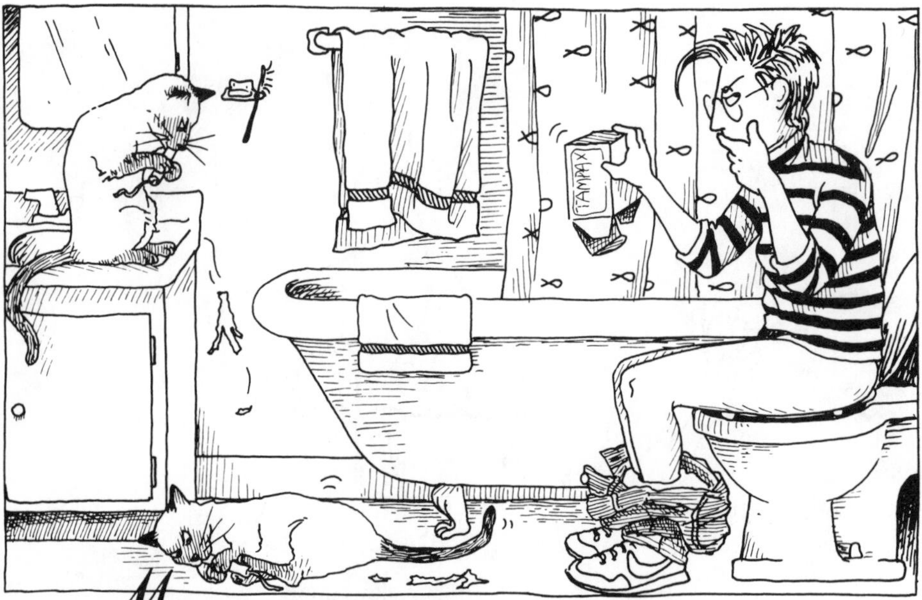
TAMPAX

MO COULD HAVE SWORN SHE HAD TWO TAMPONS LEFT.

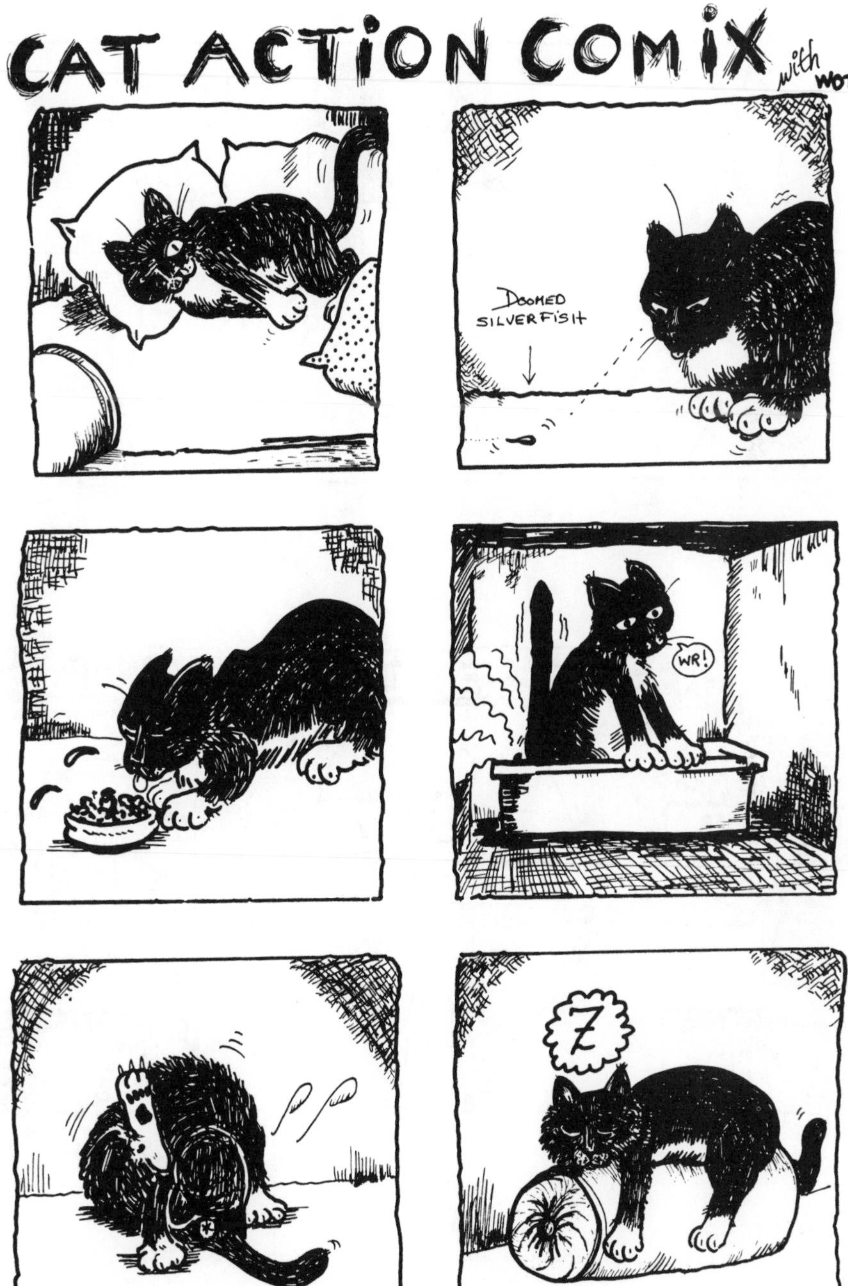
CAT ACTION COMIX with WOTAN
DOOMED SILVERFISH
WR!
Z
© L. KENNEDY '91

Marian Henley

©1988 Marian Henley

...A CAT'S COMPLETE GUIDE to HUMAN ANATOMY!
Other than the primitive functions listed here, there's really not much to it!
A. THE CAN-OPENER
B. THE AUXILIARY CAN-OPENER
SLIMY TIDBITS
C. THE SCRATCHING POSTS
SLASH
A.
B.
C.
D.
E.
©1990 Marian Henley
D. THE LANDING STRIP
OOF
and KNEADING BOARD
OOF OOF
and LAUNCH PAD
OOF
E. THE MEANINGLESS NOISEMAKER
Stop that! I said STOP THAT, You @#* CAT! Get OUT of there or I swear I'll

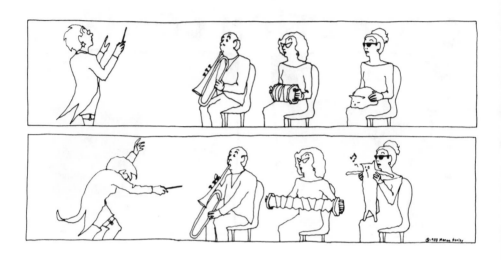

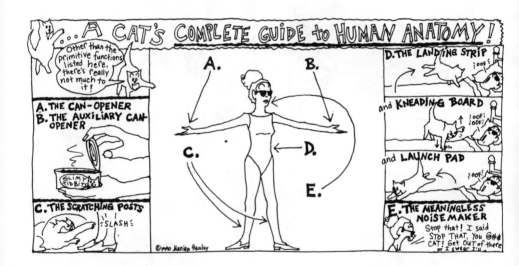

"THERE ARE TWO KINDS OF CAT FUR:
DARK FUR THAT SHEDS ON LIGHT FABRIC,
AND LIGHT FUR THAT SHEDS ON DARK FABRIC."

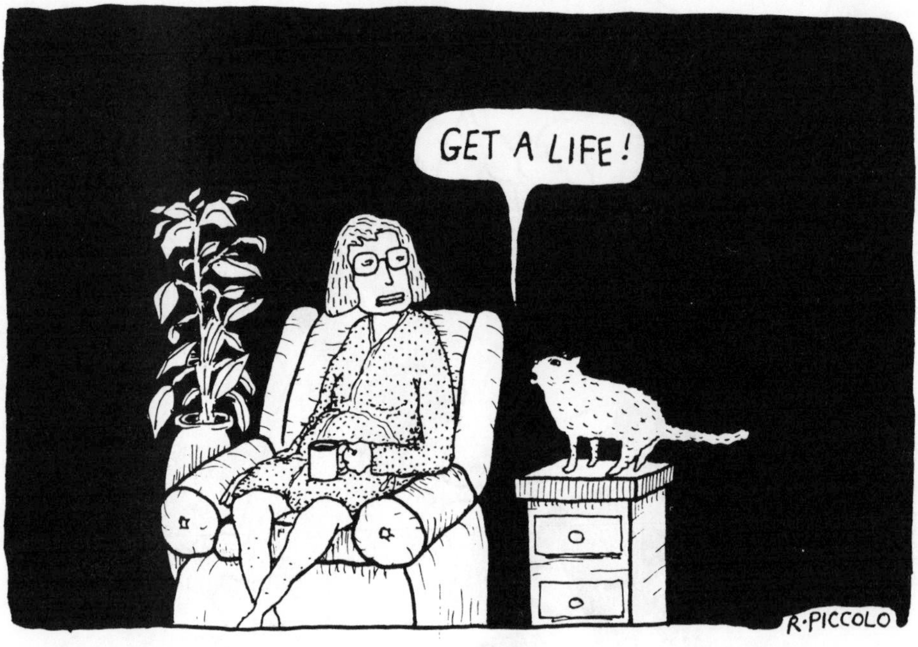
GET A LIFE!
R·PICCOLO

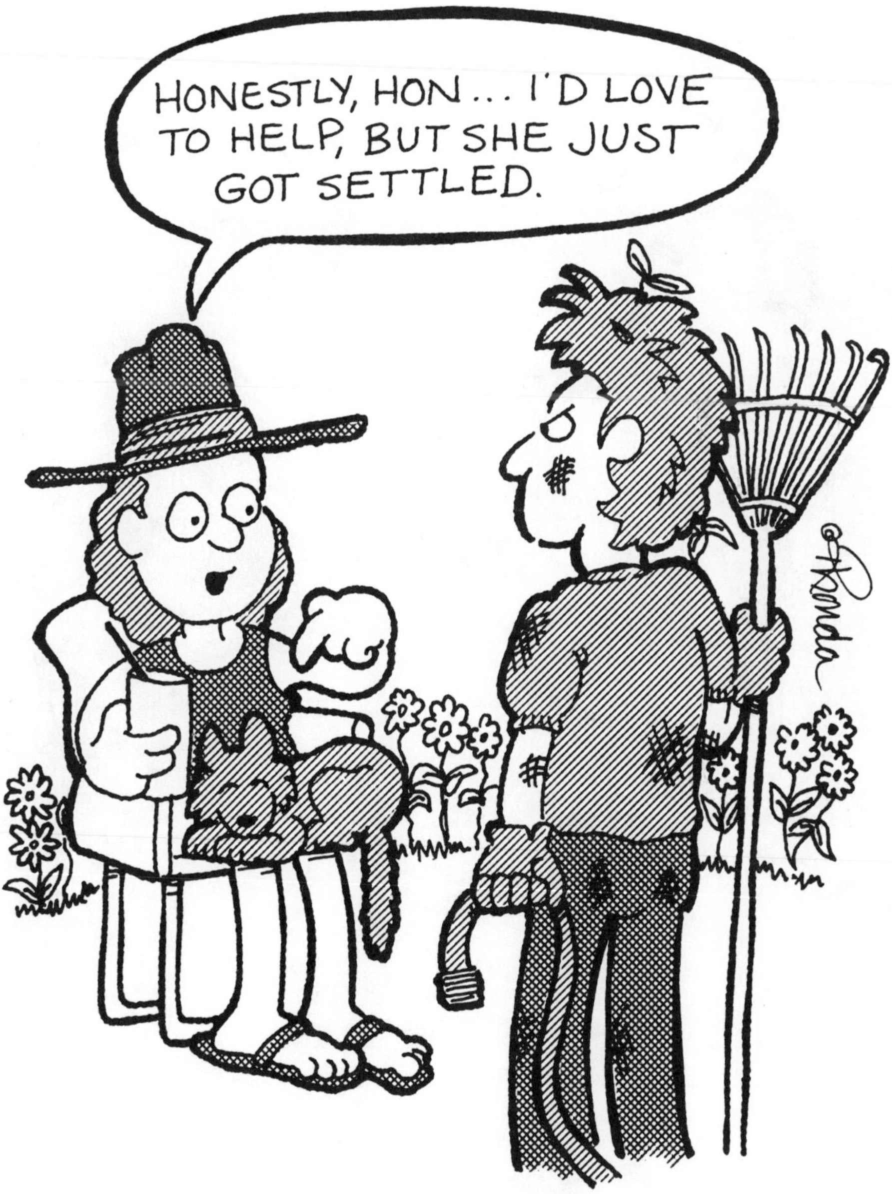
HONESTLY, HON... I'D LOVE TO HELP, BUT SHE JUST GOT SETTLED.
©Rhonda

REMOTE KITTY CONTROL

SUZY BECKER

STONEWALL RIOTS

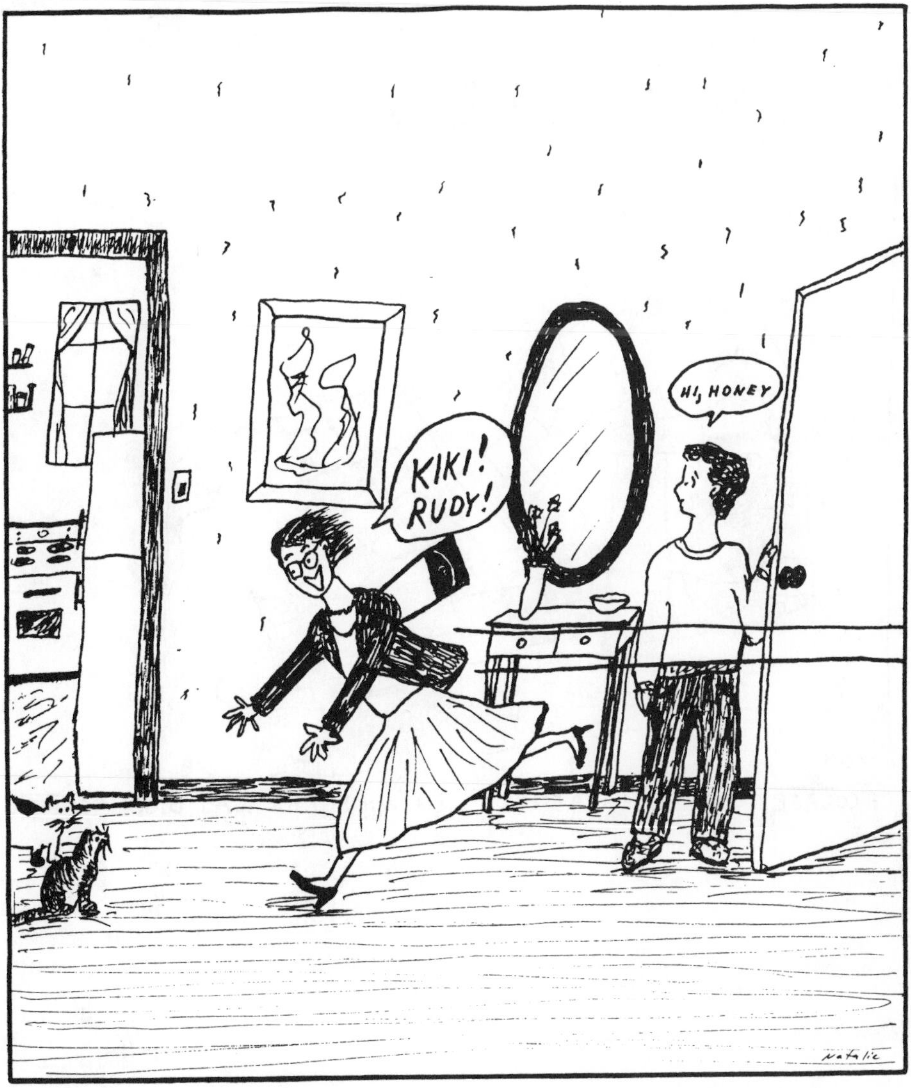
KIKI! RUDY!
HI, HONEY
Natalie

ALEXIS COULD NO LONGER DENY SHE WAS LOSING TO THE COMPETITION.

The Woman Who Knew Too Much

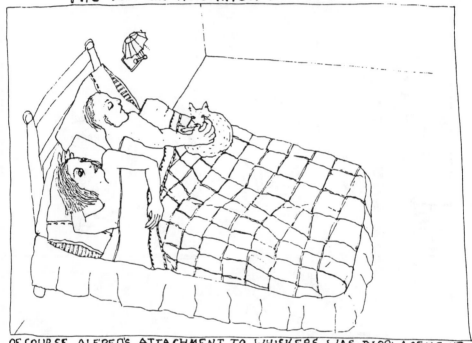

OF COURSE, ALFRED'S ATTACHMENT TO WHISKERS WAS DISPLACEMENT.

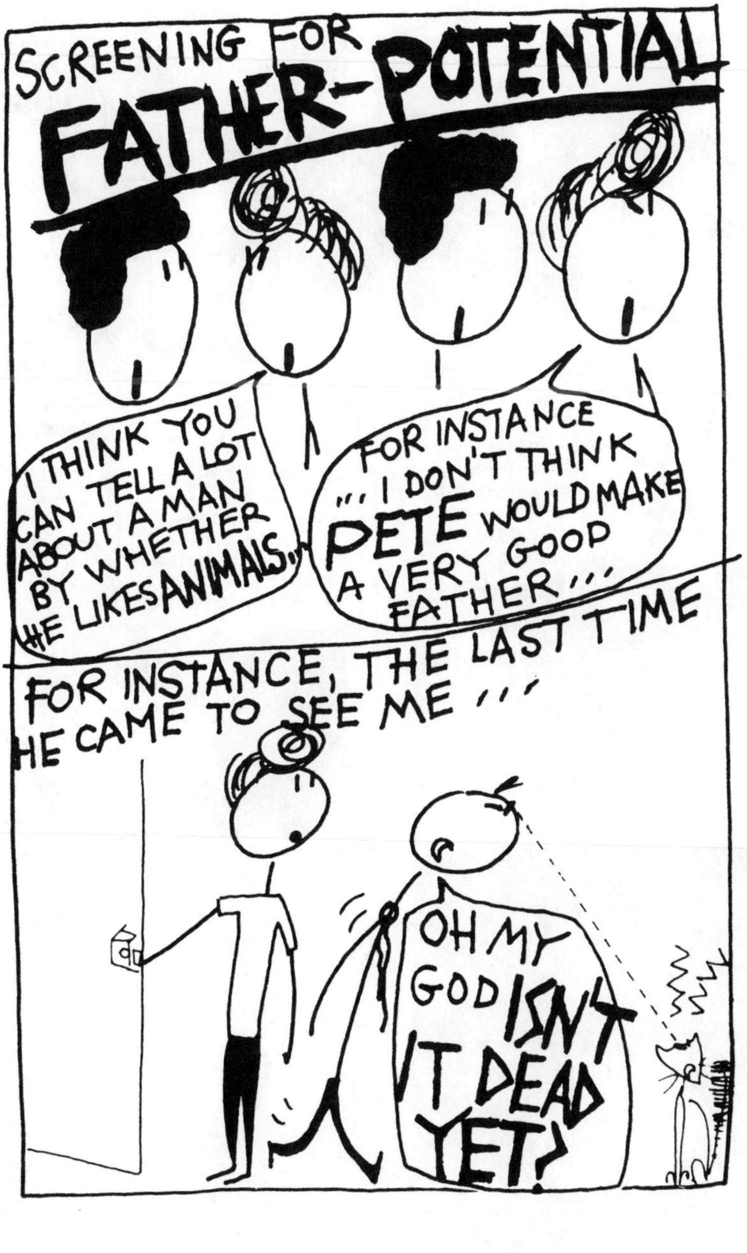
SCREENING FOR FATHER-POTENTIAL
I THINK YOU CAN TELL A LOT ABOUT A MAN BY WHETHER HE LIKES ANIMALS...
FOR INSTANCE ... I DON'T THINK PETE WOULD MAKE A VERY GOOD FATHER...
FOR INSTANCE, THE LAST TIME HE CAME TO SEE ME ...
OH MY GOD ISN'T IT DEAD YET?

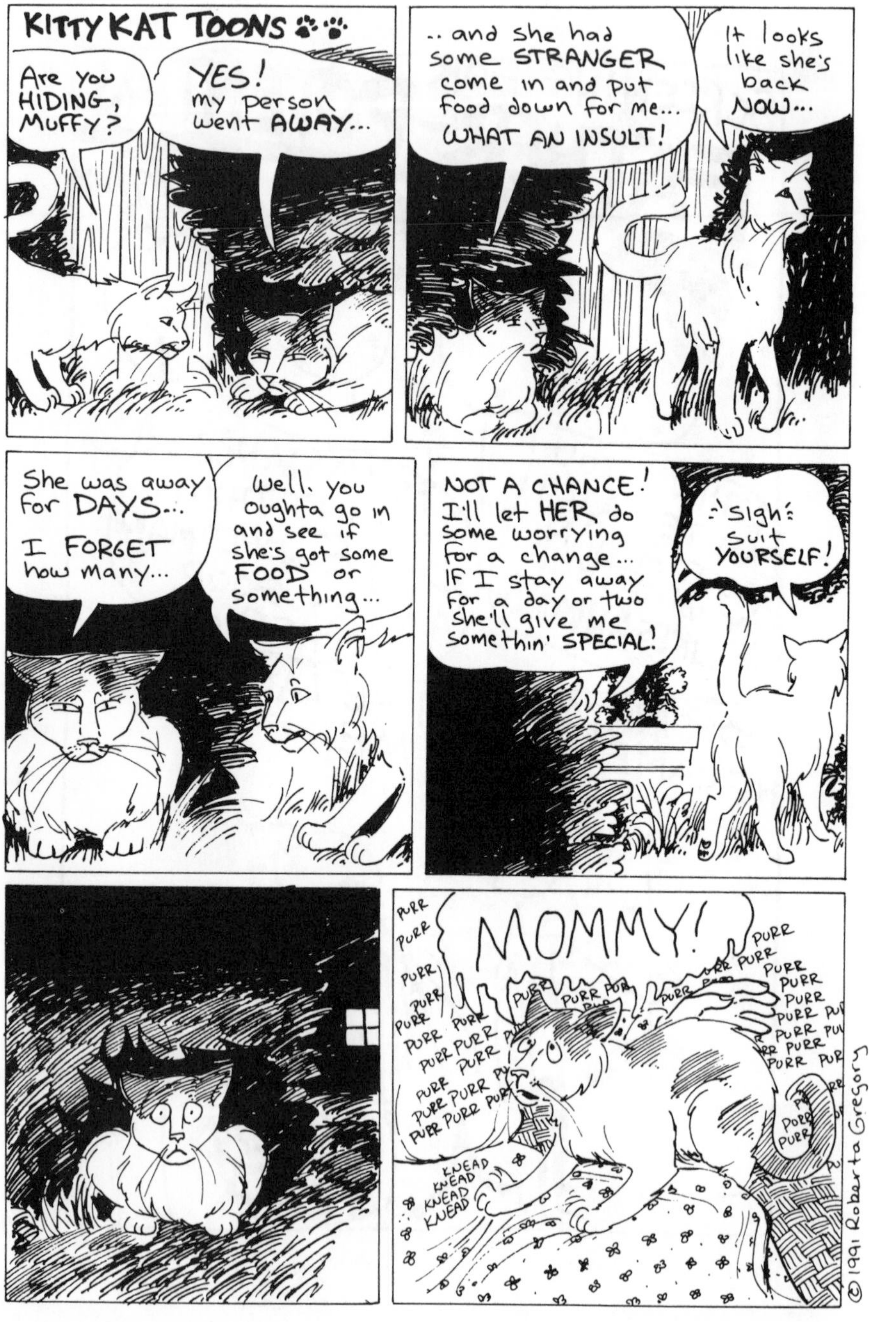
KITTY KAT TOONS
Are you HIDING, MUFFY?
YES! my person went AWAY...
.. and she had some STRANGER come in and put food down for me... WHAT AN INSULT!
It looks like she's back NOW...
She was away for DAYS... I FORGET how many...
Well, you oughta go in and see if she's got some FOOD or something...
NOT A CHANCE! I'll let HER do some worrying for a change... If I stay away for a day or two she'll give me somethin' SPECIAL!
Sigh Suit YOURSELF!
MOMMY!
PURR PURR PURR PURR PURR PURR PURR PURR PURR
KNEAD KNEAD KNEAD KNEAD
© 1991 Roberta Gregory

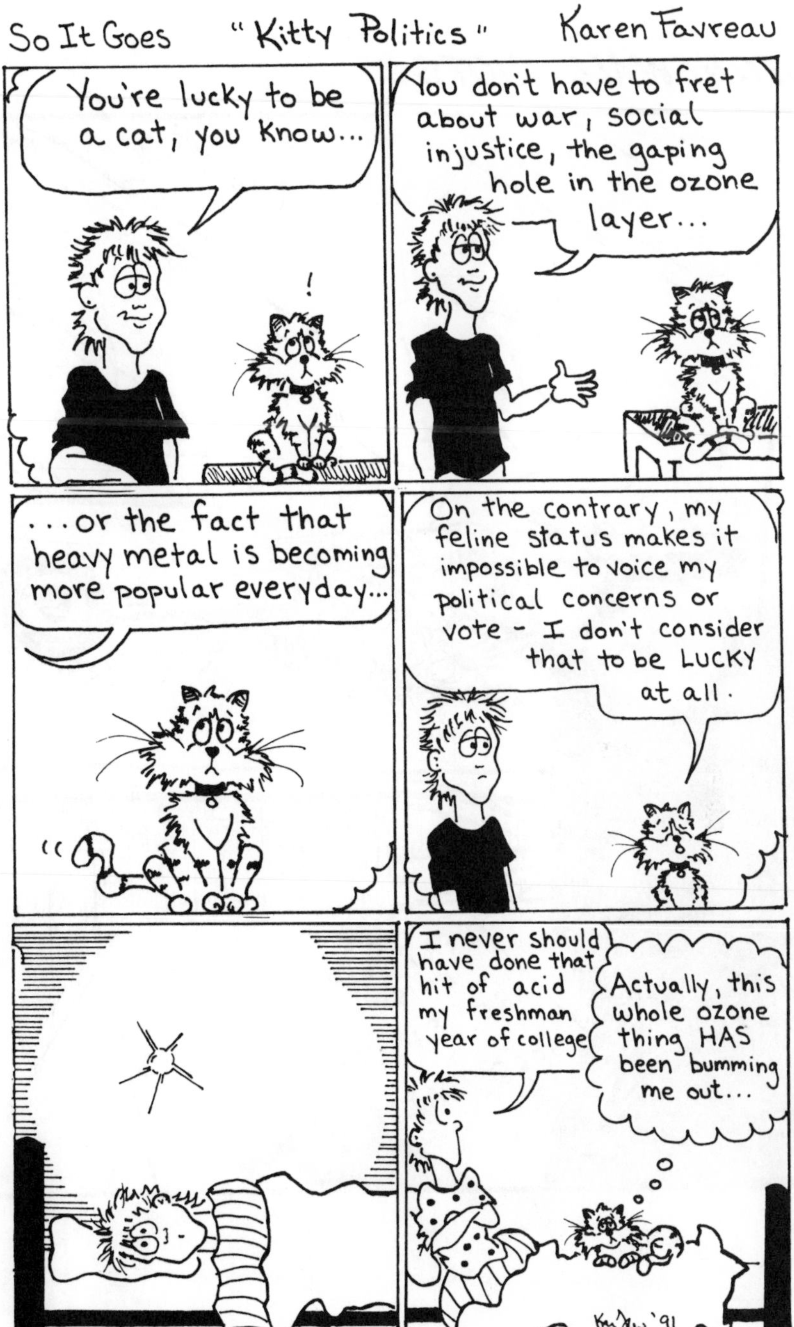
So It Goes
"Kitty Politics"
Karen Favreau
You're lucky to be a cat, you know...
!
You don't have to fret about war, social injustice, the gaping hole in the ozone layer...
...or the fact that heavy metal is becoming more popular everyday...
On the contrary, my feline status makes it impossible to voice my political concerns or vote - I don't consider that to be LUCKY at all.
I never should have done that hit of acid my freshman year of college
Actually, this whole ozone thing HAS been bumming me out...
'91

STONEWALL RIOTS

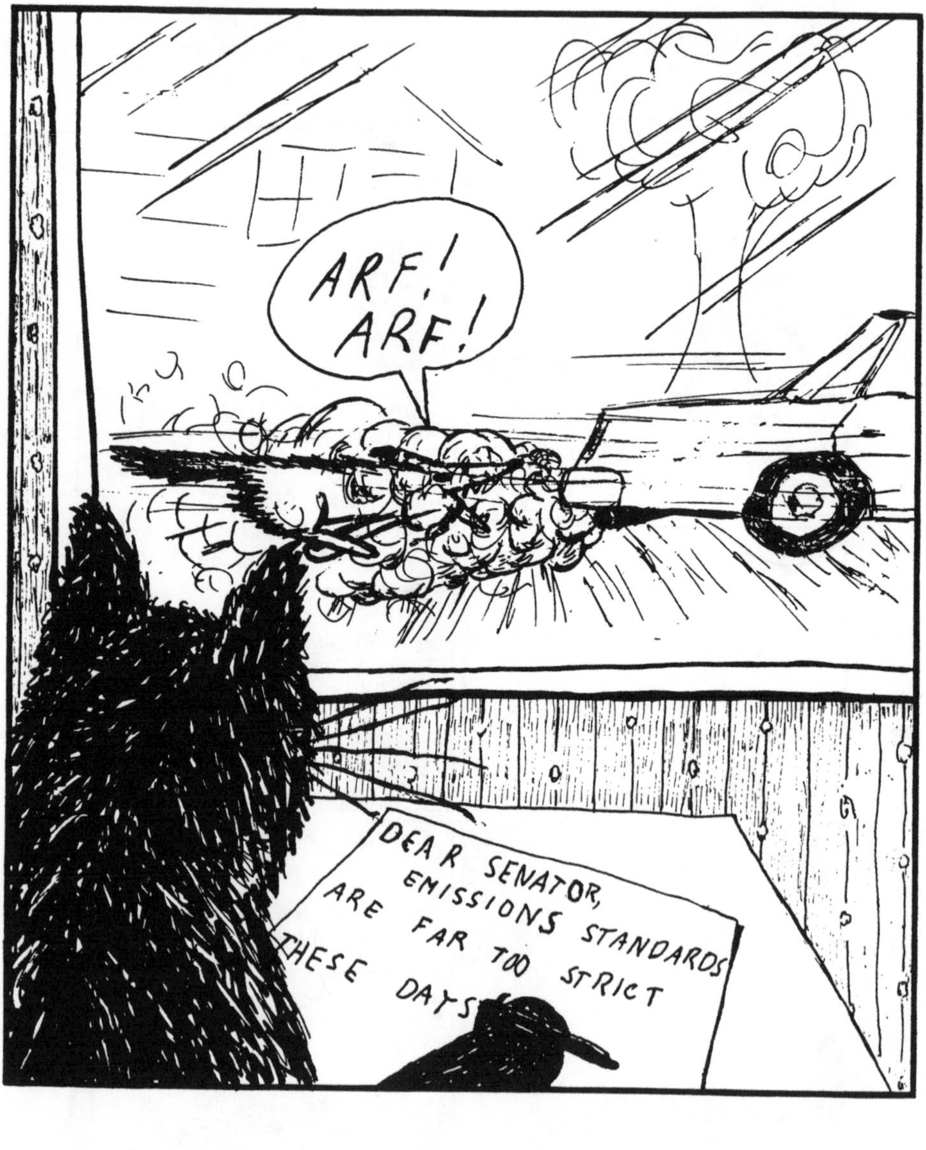
ARF! ARF!
DEAR SENATOR, EMISSIONS STANDARDS ARE FAR TOO STRICT THESE DAYS

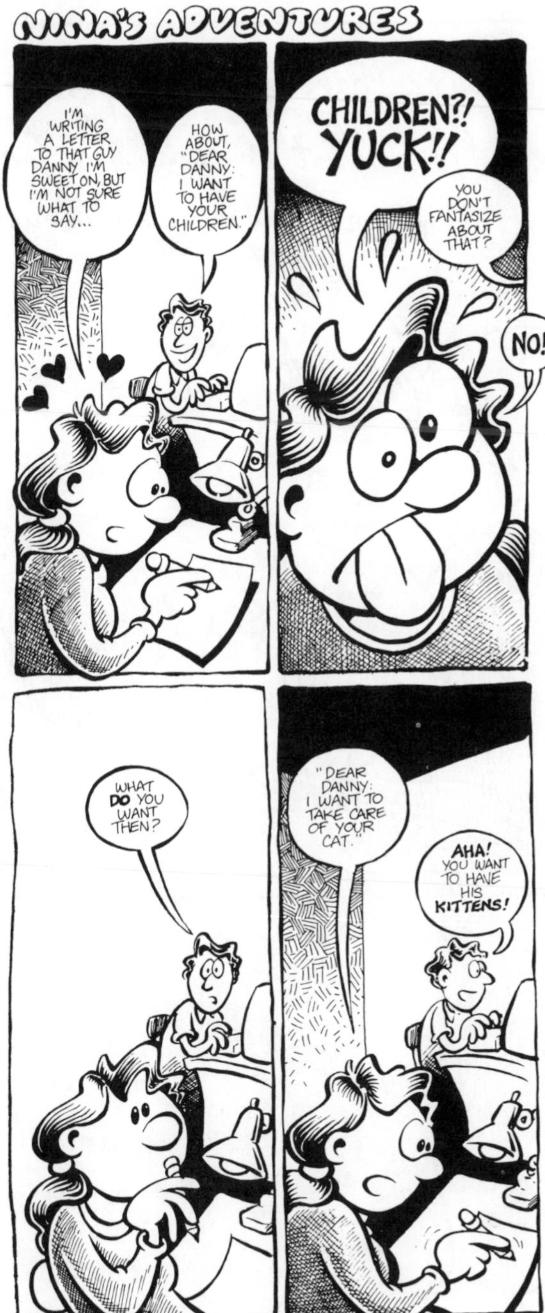
NINA'S ADVENTURES
I'M WRITING A LETTER TO THAT GUY DANNY I'M SWEET ON, BUT I'M NOT SURE WHAT TO SAY...
HOW ABOUT, "DEAR DANNY: I WANT TO HAVE YOUR CHILDREN."
CHILDREN?! YUCK!!
YOU DON'T FANTASIZE ABOUT THAT?
NO!
WHAT DO YOU WANT THEN?
"DEAR DANNY: I WANT TO TAKE CARE OF YOUR CAT."
AHA! YOU WANT TO HAVE HIS KITTENS!
© NINA PALEY 9-5-91

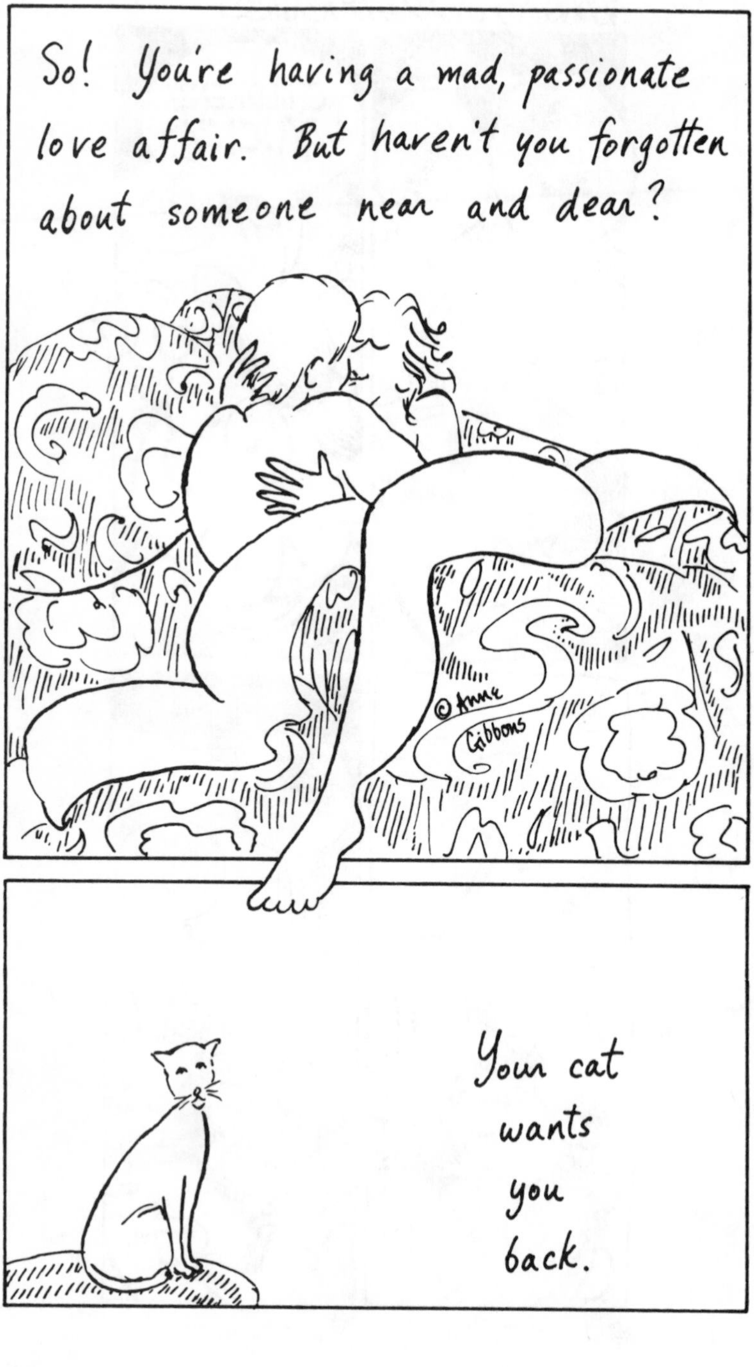
So! You're having a mad, passionate love affair. But haven't you forgotten about someone near and dear?
© Anne Gibbons
Your cat wants you back.

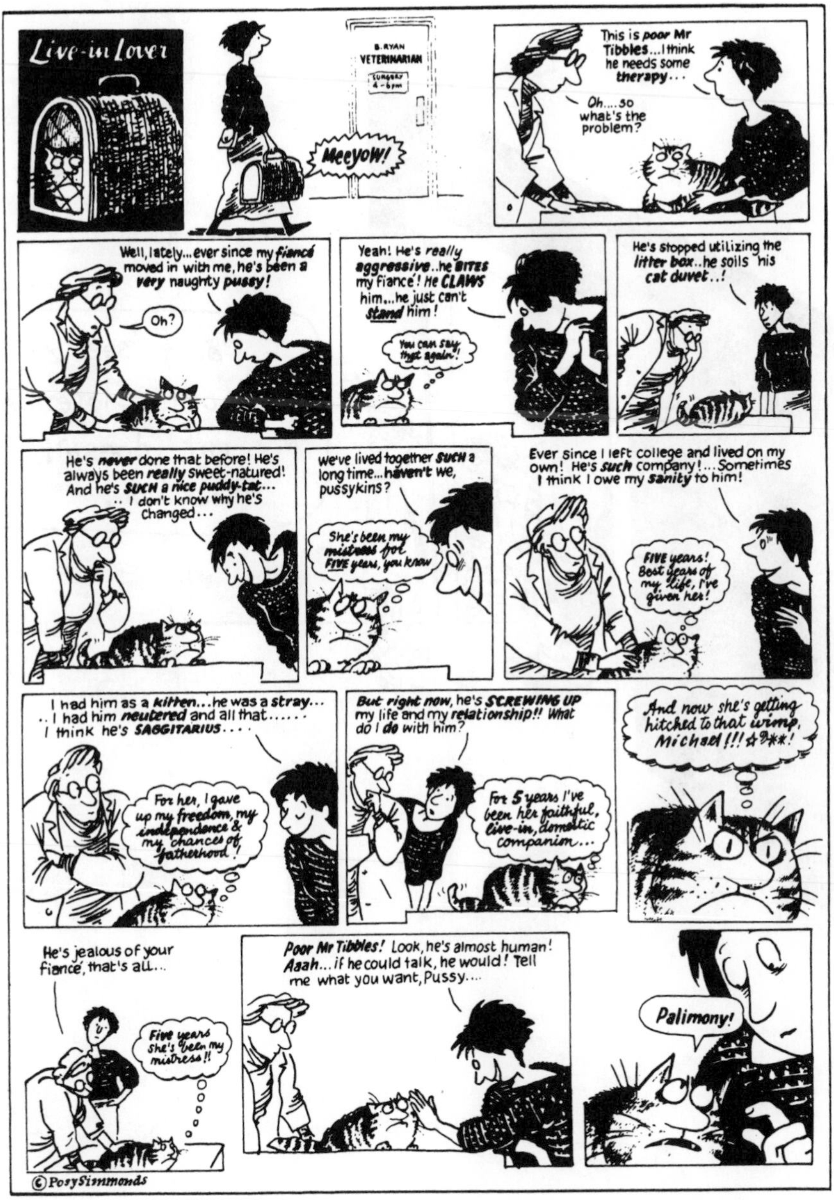

Live-in Lover
B. RYAN
VETERINARIAN
SURGERY 4 - 6pm
MeeyoW!
This is poor Mr Tibbles...I think he needs some therapy...
Oh....so what's the problem?
Well, lately...ever since my fiancé moved in with me, he's been a very naughty pussy!
Oh?
Yeah! He's really aggressive..he BITES my fiancé! He CLAWS him...he just can't stand him!
You can say that again!
He's stopped utilizing the litter box..he soils his cat duvet..!
He's never done that before! He's always been really sweet-natured! And he's SUCH a nice puddy-tat... .. I don't know why he's changed...
We've lived together SUCH a long time...haven't we, pussykins?
She's been my mistress for FIVE years, you know
Ever since I left college and lived on my own! He's such company!...Sometimes I think I owe my sanity to him!
FIVE years! Best years of my life, I've given her!
I had him as a kitten...he was a stray... ..I had him neutered and all that...... I think he's SAGGITARIUS....
For her, I gave up my freedom, my independence & my chances of fatherhood!
But right now, he's SCREWING UP my life and my relationship!! What do I do with him?
For 5 years I've been her faithful, live-in, domestic companion...
And now she's getting hitched to that wimp, Michael!!!
He's jealous of your fiancé, that's all...
Five years she's been my mistress!!
Poor Mr Tibbles! Look, he's almost human! Aaah...if he could talk, he would! Tell me what you want, Pussy...
Palimony!
© Posy Simmonds

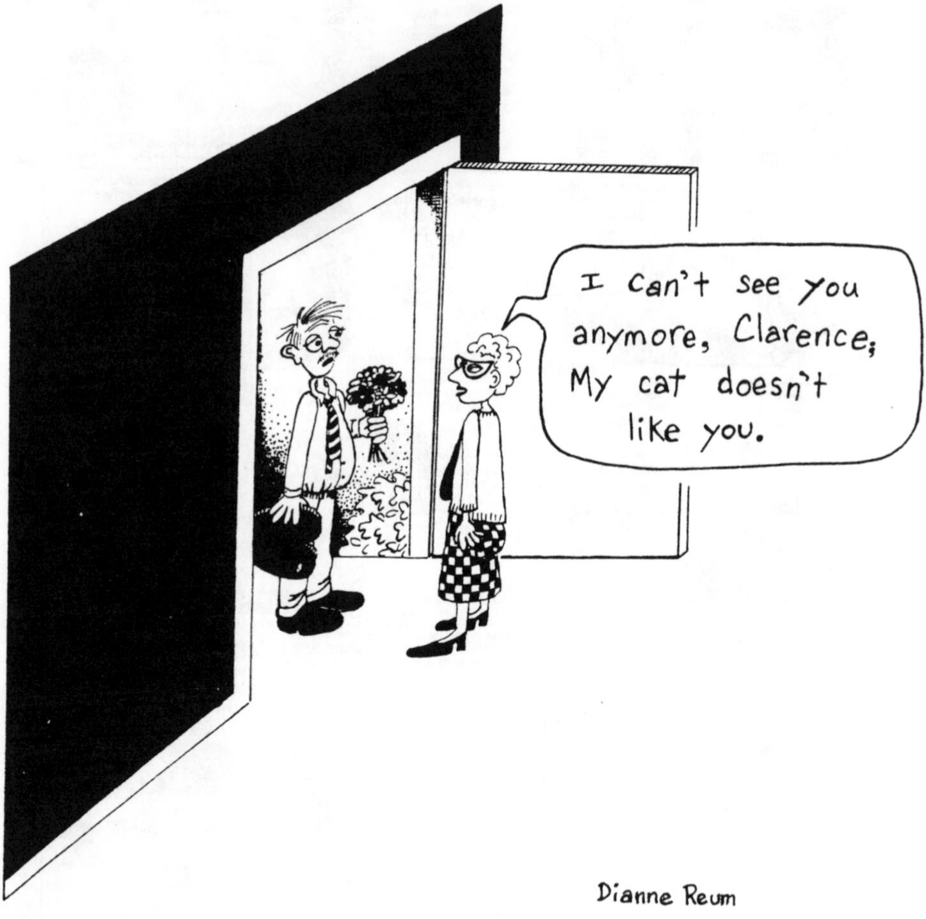
I can't see you anymore, Clarence; My cat doesn't like you.
Dianne Reum

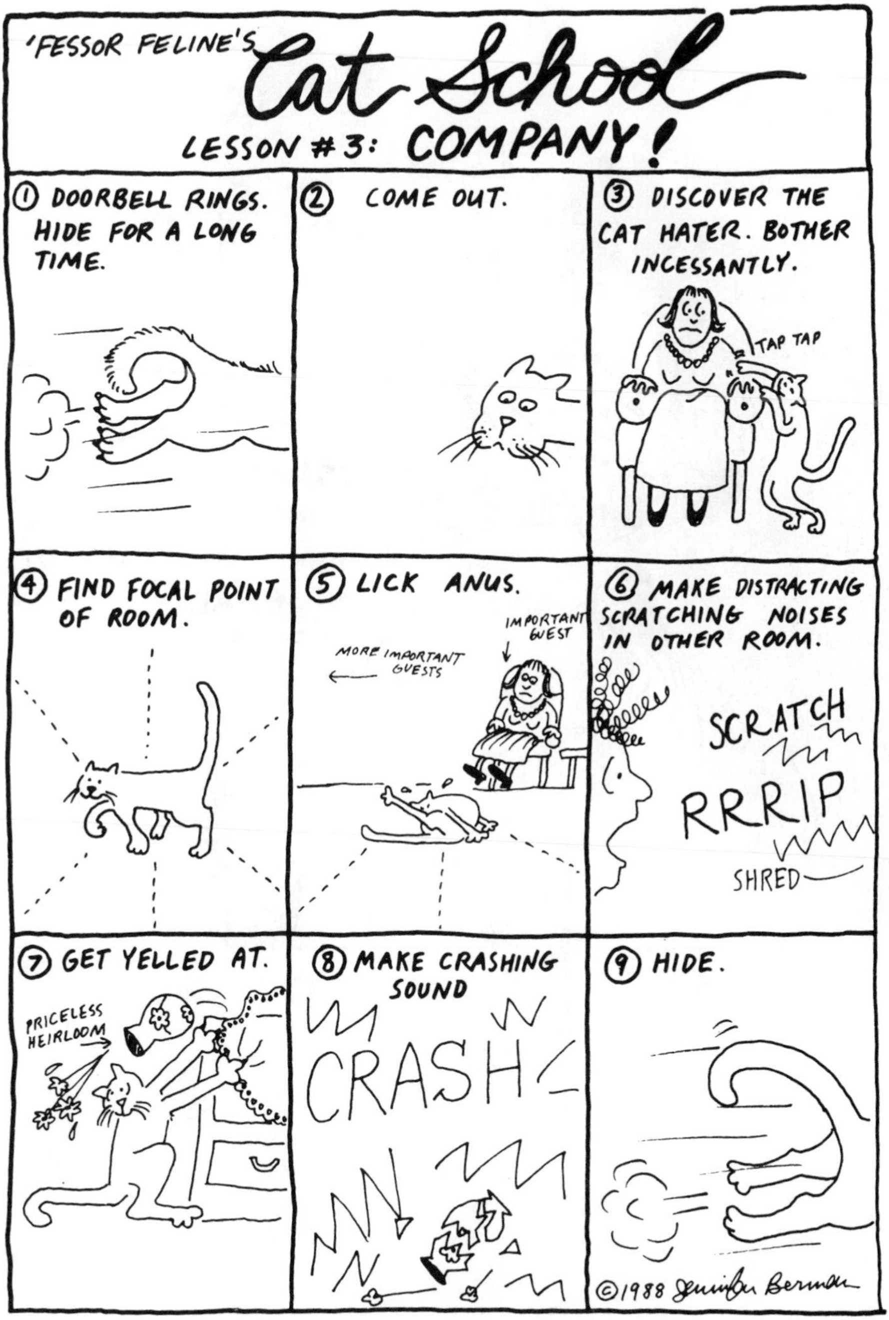
'FESSOR FELINE'S Cat School
LESSON #3: COMPANY!
① DOORBELL RINGS. HIDE FOR A LONG TIME.
② COME OUT.
③ DISCOVER THE CAT HATER. BOTHER INCESSANTLY.
TAP TAP
④ FIND FOCAL POINT OF ROOM.
⑤ LICK ANUS.
IMPORTANT GUEST
MORE IMPORTANT GUESTS
⑥ MAKE DISTRACTING SCRATCHING NOISES IN OTHER ROOM.
SCRATCH
RRRIP
SHRED
⑦ GET YELLED AT.
PRICELESS HEIRLOOM
⑧ MAKE CRASHING SOUND
CRASH
⑨ HIDE.
©1988 Jennifer Berman

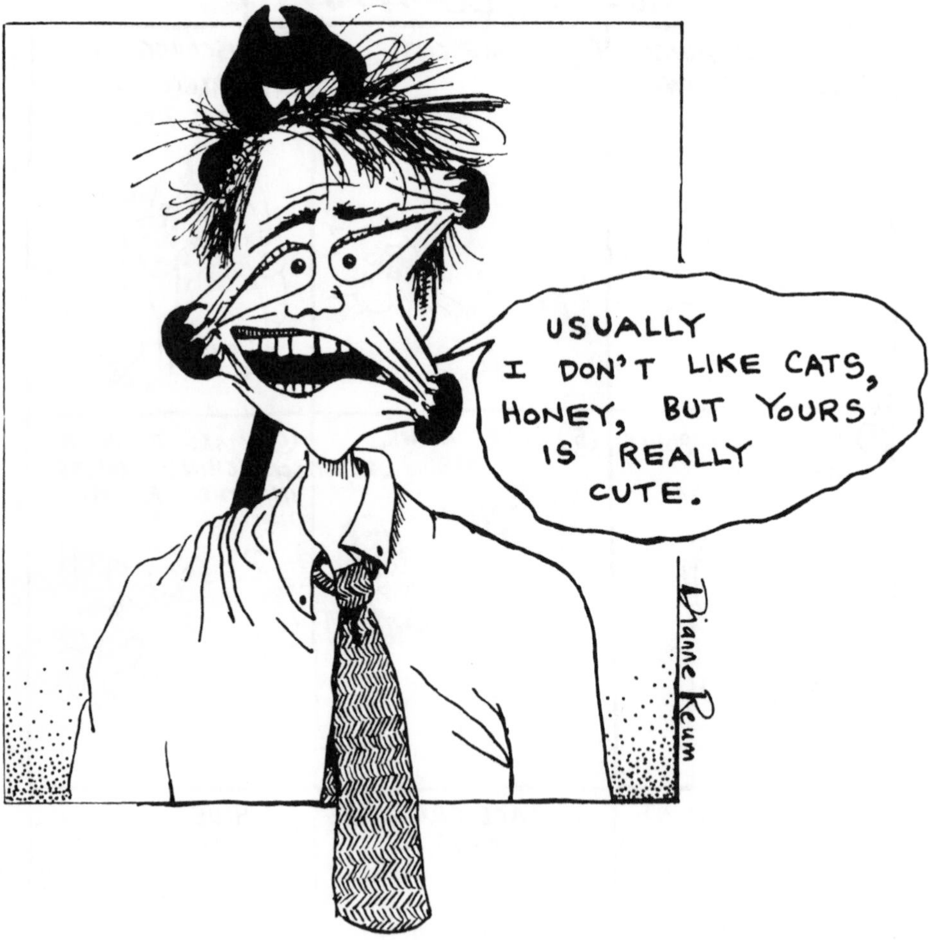
USUALLY I DON'T LIKE CATS, HONEY, BUT YOURS IS REALLY CUTE.
Dianne Reum

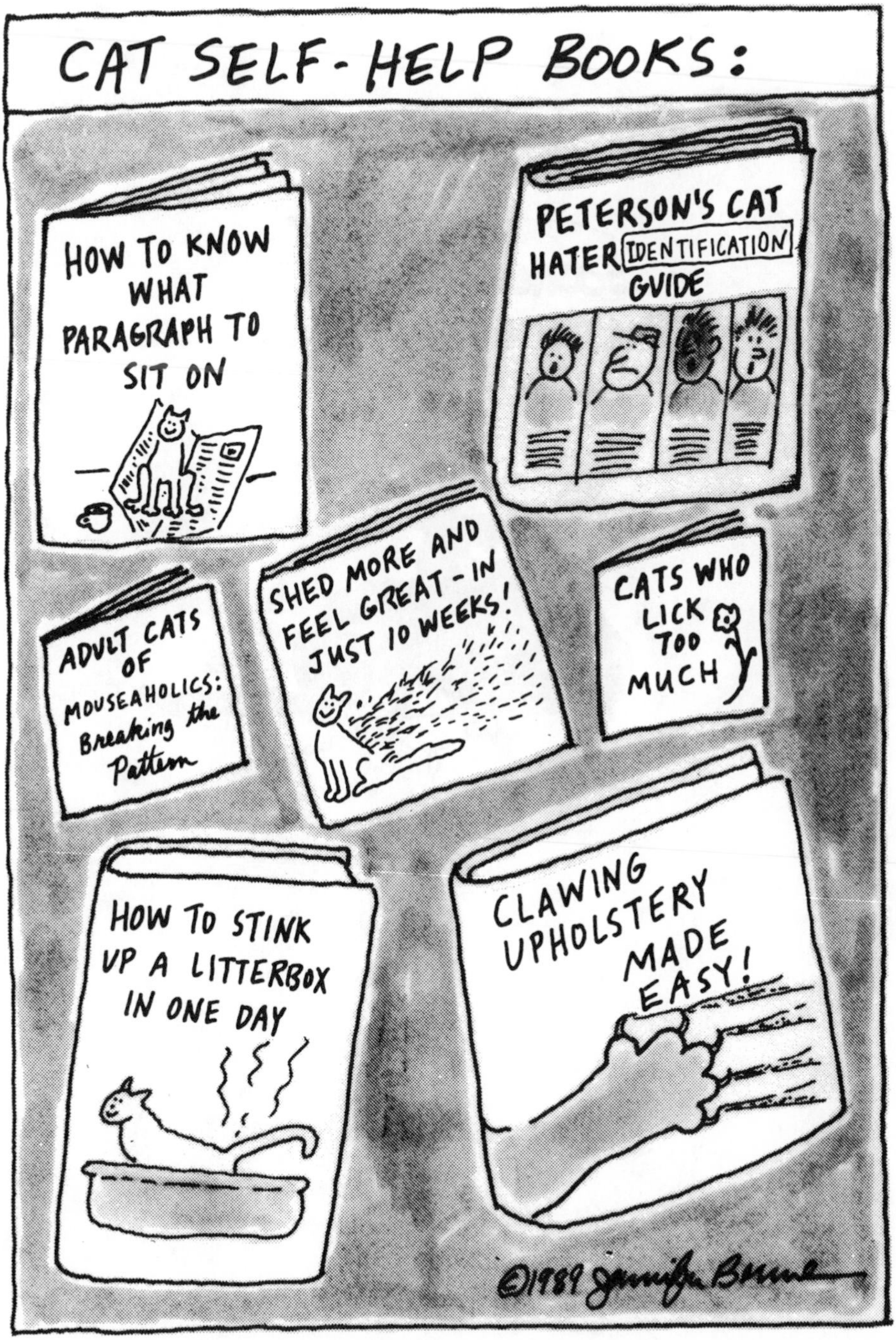
CAT SELF-HELP BOOKS:
HOW TO KNOW WHAT PARAGRAPH TO SIT ON
PETERSON'S CAT HATER IDENTIFICATION GUIDE
ADULT CATS OF MOUSEAHOLICS: Breaking the Pattern
SHED MORE AND FEEL GREAT - IN JUST 10 WEEKS!
CATS WHO LICK TOO MUCH
HOW TO STINK UP A LITTERBOX IN ONE DAY
CLAWING UPHOLSTERY MADE EASY!
©1989 Jennifer Berman

Sooner or later
Mother always gets
the blame
VQ.

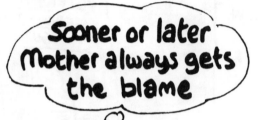

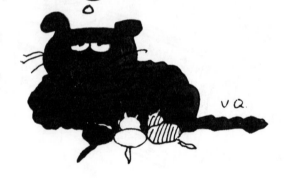

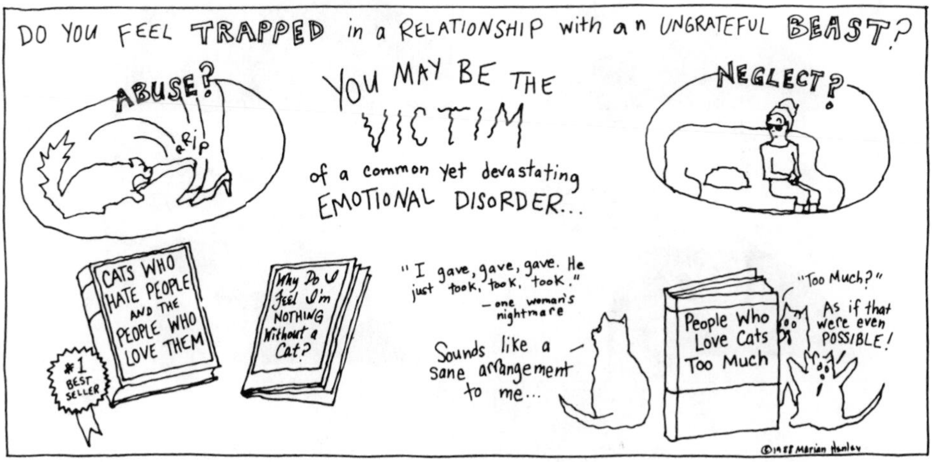
DO YOU FEEL TRAPPED in a RELATIONSHIP with an UNGRATEFUL BEAST?
ABUSE?
RIP
YOU MAY BE THE VICTIM of a common yet devastating EMOTIONAL DISORDER...
NEGLECT?
CATS WHO HATE PEOPLE AND THE PEOPLE WHO LOVE THEM
#1 BEST SELLER
Why Do I Feel I'm NOTHING Without a Cat?
"I gave, gave, gave. He just took, took, took." —one woman's nightmare
Sounds like a sane arrangement to me...
People Who Love Cats Too Much
"Too Much?"
As if that were even POSSIBLE!
©1988 Marian Henley

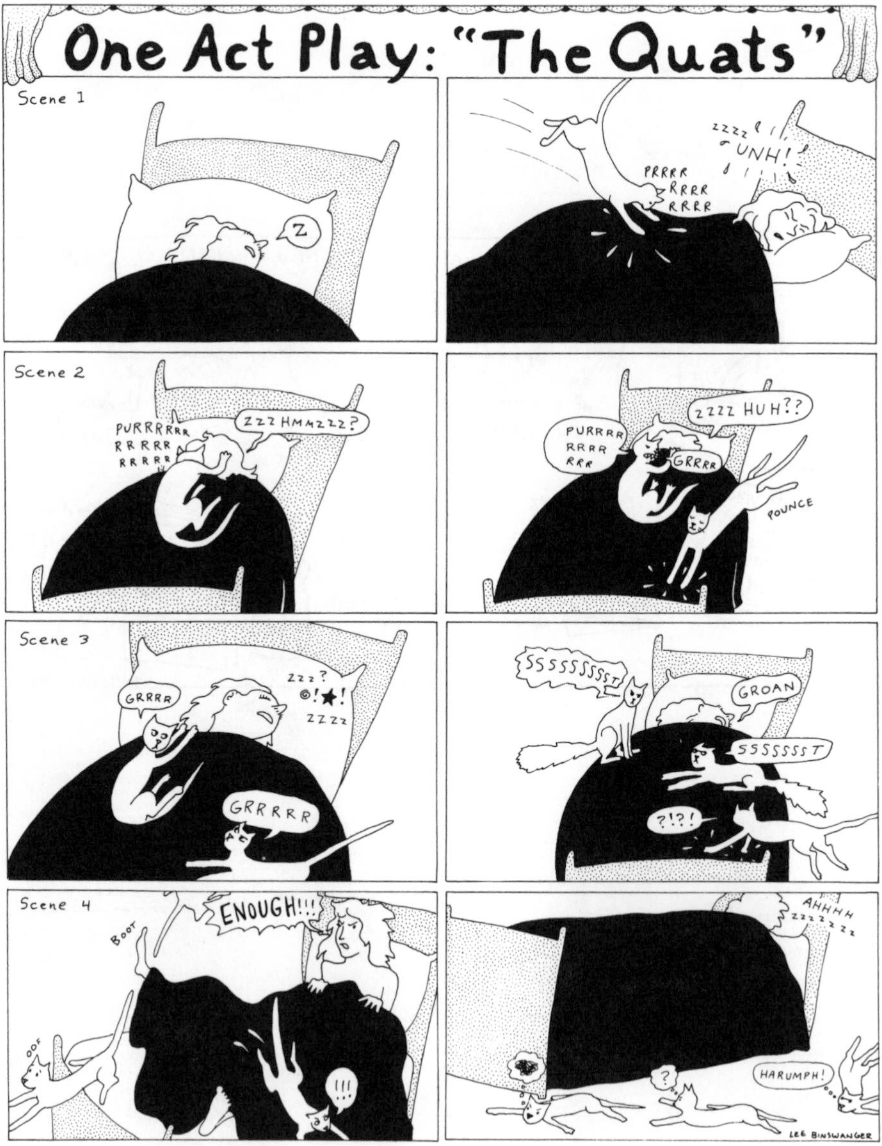
One Act Play: "The Quats"
Scene 1
Z
PRRRR RRRR RRRR
ZZZZ UNH!
Scene 2
PURRRRRRR RRRRR RRRRR
ZZZ HMMZZZ?
PURRRR RRRR RRR
ZZZZ HUH??
GRRRR
POUNCE
Scene 3
GRRRR
ZZZ? ©!★!
ZZZZ
GRRRRR
SSSSSSSSST
GROAN
SSSSSSST
?!?!
Scene 4
BOOT
ENOUGH!!!
OOF
!!!
AHHHH ZZZZZZZ
?
HARUMPH!
LEE BINSWANGER

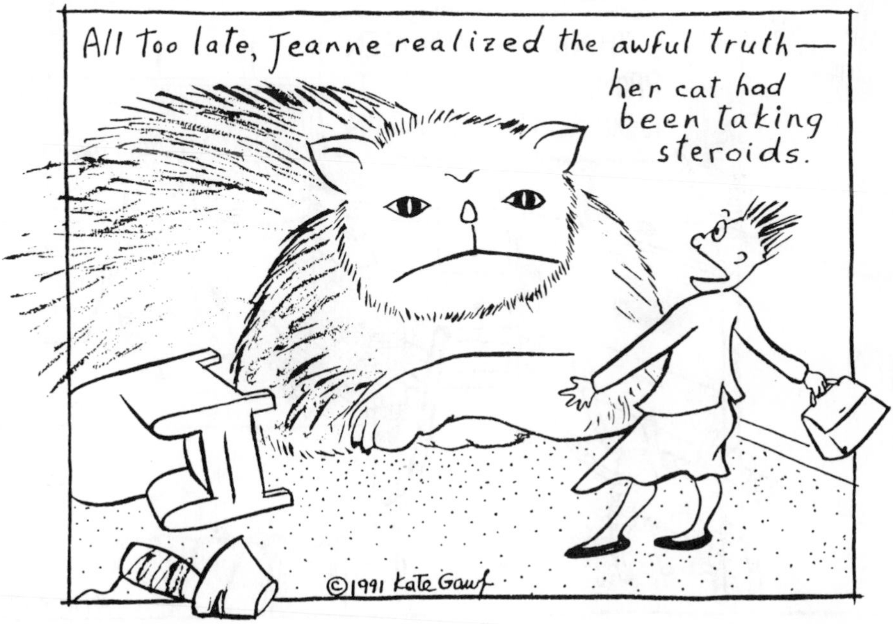
All too late, Jeanne realized the awful truth—
her cat had been taking steroids.
©1991 Kate Gawf

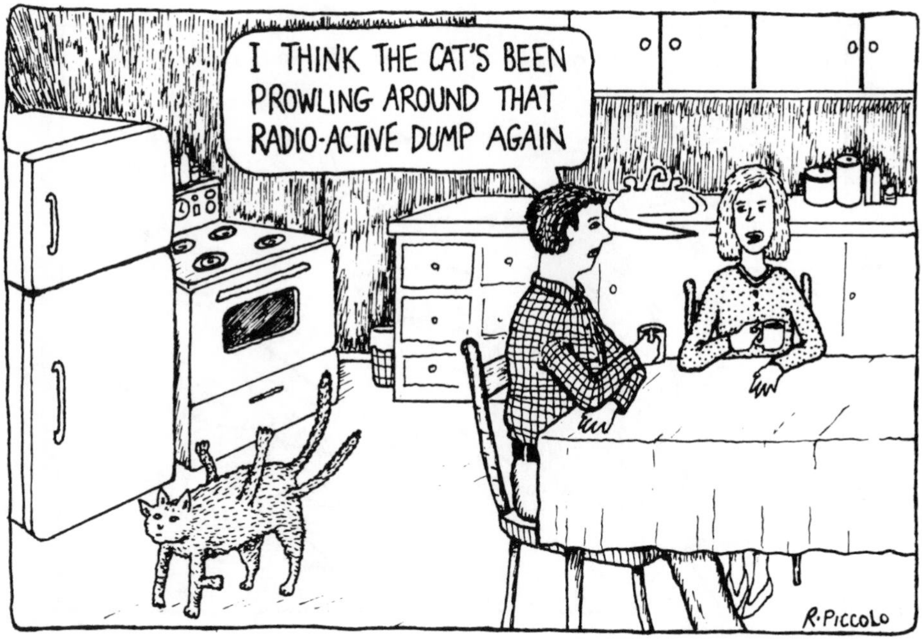
I THINK THE CAT'S BEEN PROWLING AROUND THAT RADIO-ACTIVE DUMP AGAIN
R·PICCOLO

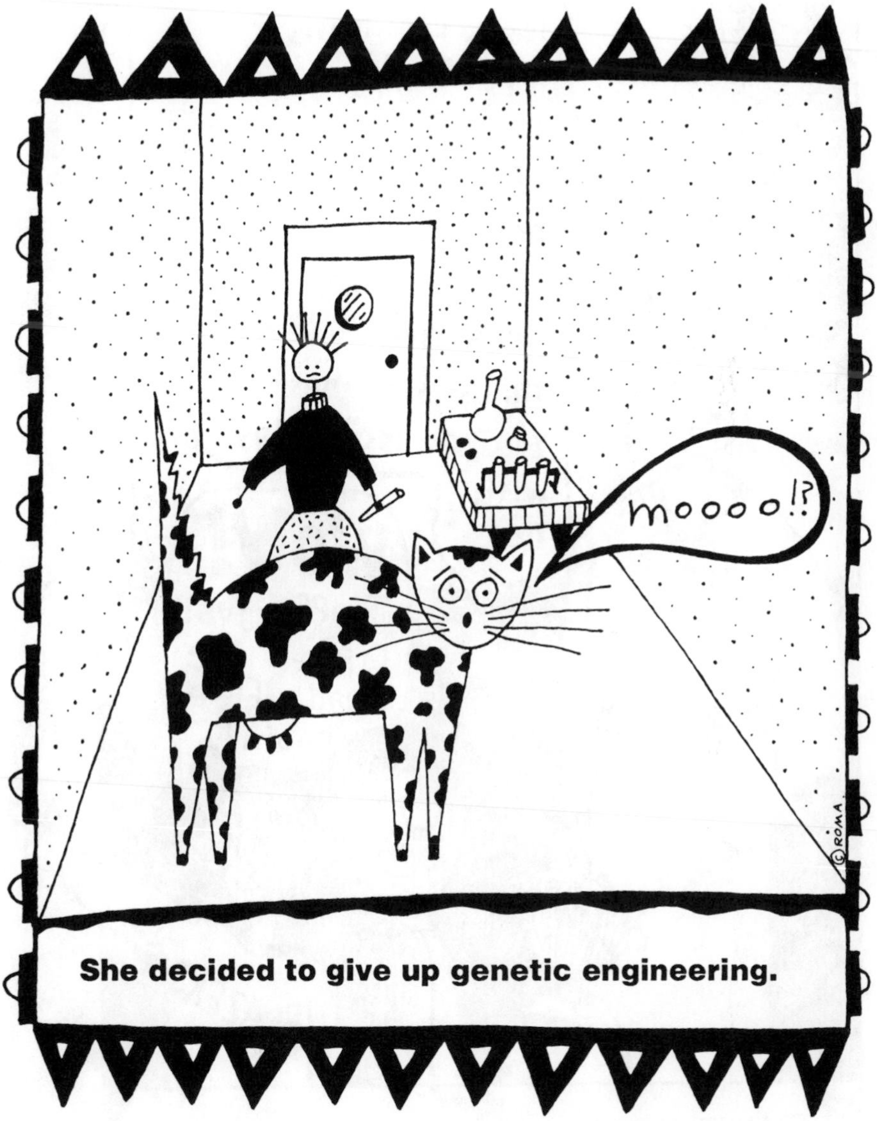
moooo!?
©ROMA

She decided to give up genetic engineering.

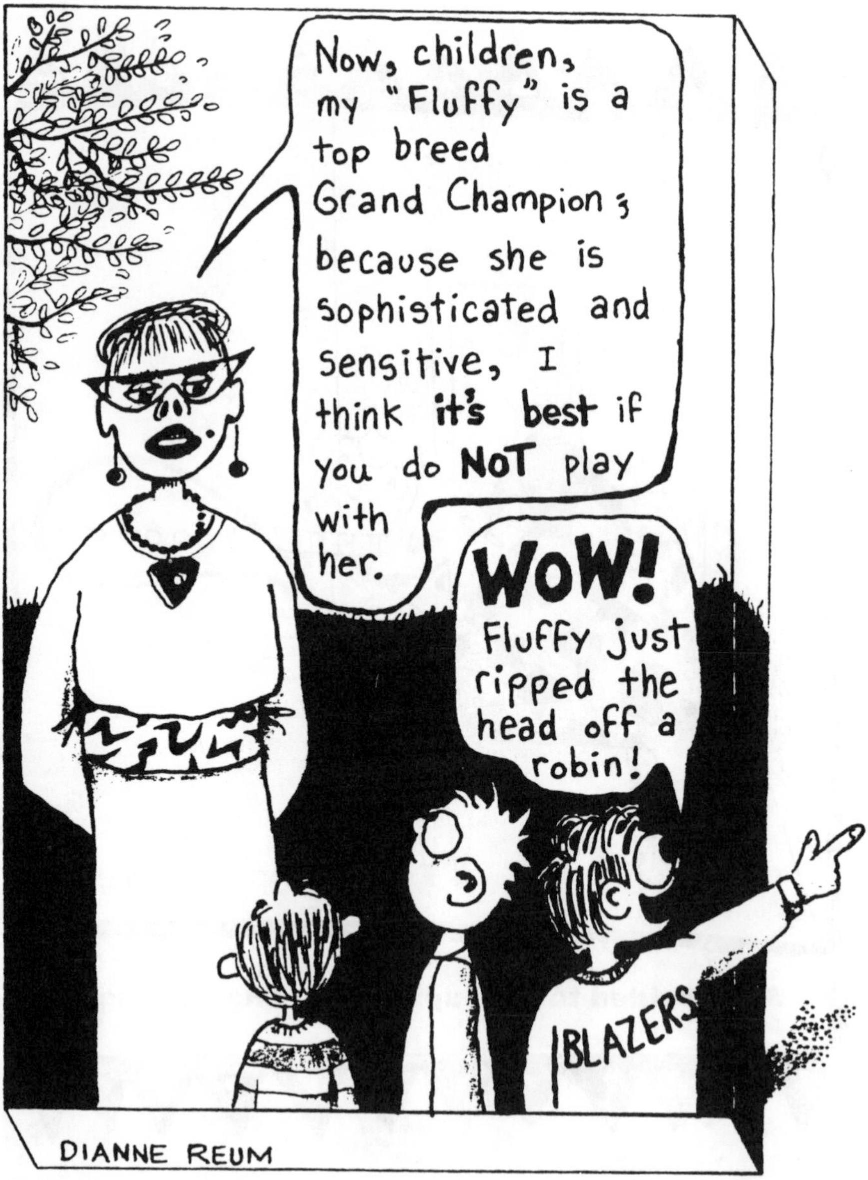
Now, children, my "Fluffy" is a top breed Grand Champion; because she is sophisticated and sensitive, I think **it's best** if you do **NOT** play with her.
WOW! Fluffy just ripped the head off a robin!
BLAZERS
DIANNE REUM

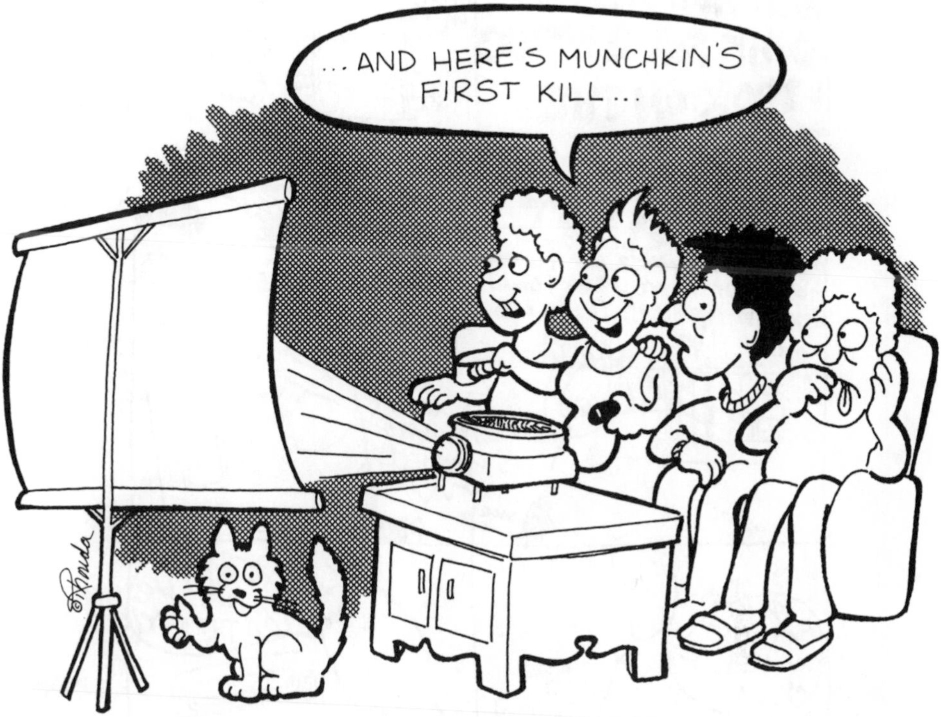
...AND HERE'S MUNCHKIN'S FIRST KILL...
Rhonda

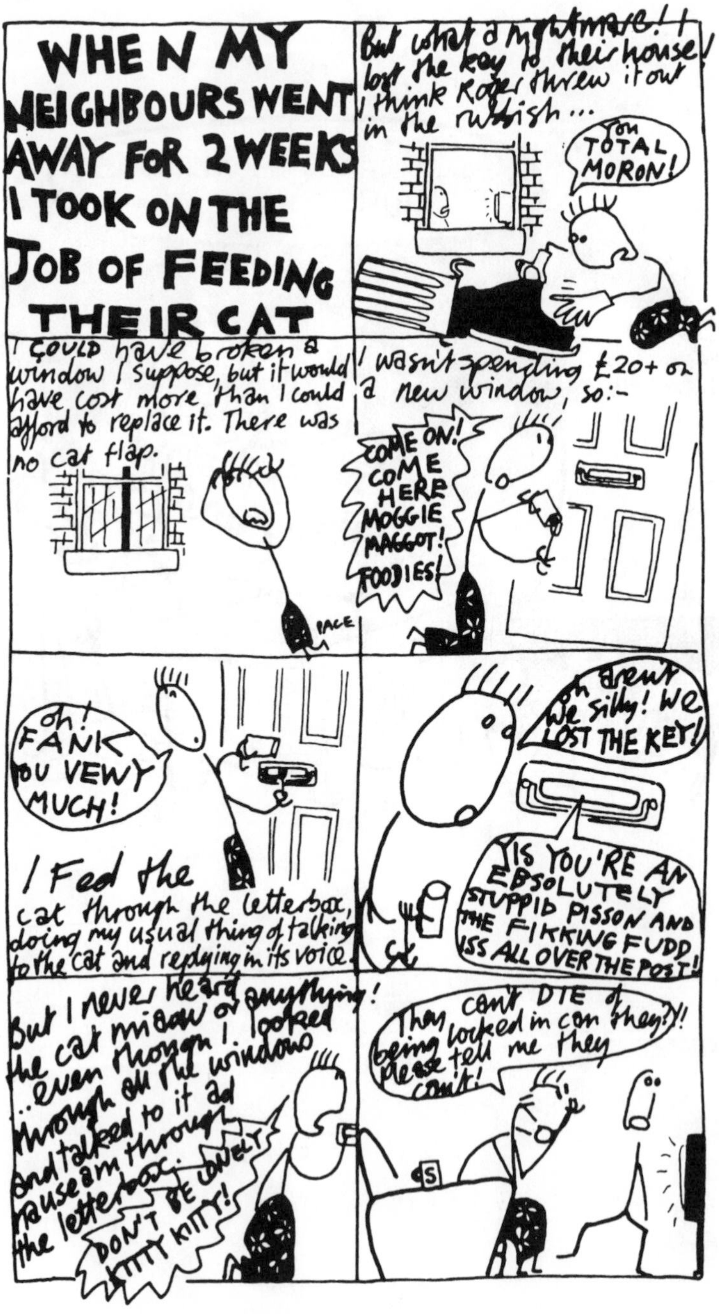
WHEN MY NEIGHBOURS WENT AWAY FOR 2 WEEKS I TOOK ON THE JOB OF FEEDING THEIR CAT
But what a nightmare!! I lost the key to their house! I think Roger threw it out in the rubbish...
You TOTAL MORON!
I COULD have broken a window I suppose, but it would have cost more than I could afford to replace it. There was no cat flap.
PACE
I wasn't spending £20+ on a new window, so:-
COME ON! COME HERE MOGGIE MAGGOT! FOODIES!
Oh! FANK YOU VEWY MUCH!
I Fed the cat through the letterbox, doing my usual thing of talking to the cat and replying in its voice.
Oh aren't we silly! We LOST THE KEY!
YIS YOU'RE AN EBSOLUTELY STUPPID PISSON AND THE FIKKING FUDD ISS ALL OVER THE POST!
But I never heard anything! the cat miaow or ... even though I looked through all the windows and talked to it and ... through the letterbox.
DON'T BE LONELY KITTY KITTY!
They can't DIE of being locked in can they?!! please tell me they can't!

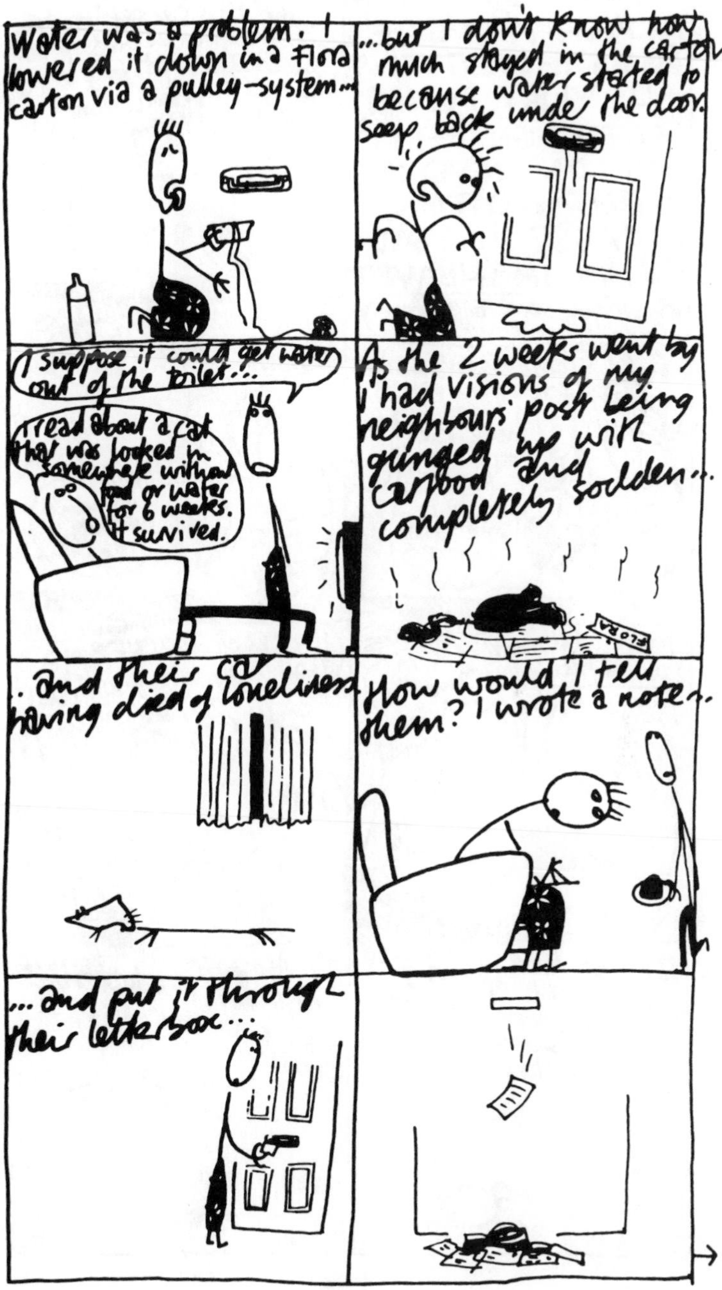
Water was a problem. I lowered it down in a Flora carton via a pulley-system...
...but I don't know how much stayed in the carton because water started to seep back unde the door.
I suppose it could get water out of the toilet...
I read about a cat that was locked in somewhere without food or water for 6 weeks. It survived.
As the 2 weeks went by I had visions of my neighbours' post being gunged up with catfood and completely sodden...
FLORA
...and their cat having died of loneliness.
How would I tell them? I wrote a note...
...and put it through their letterbox...

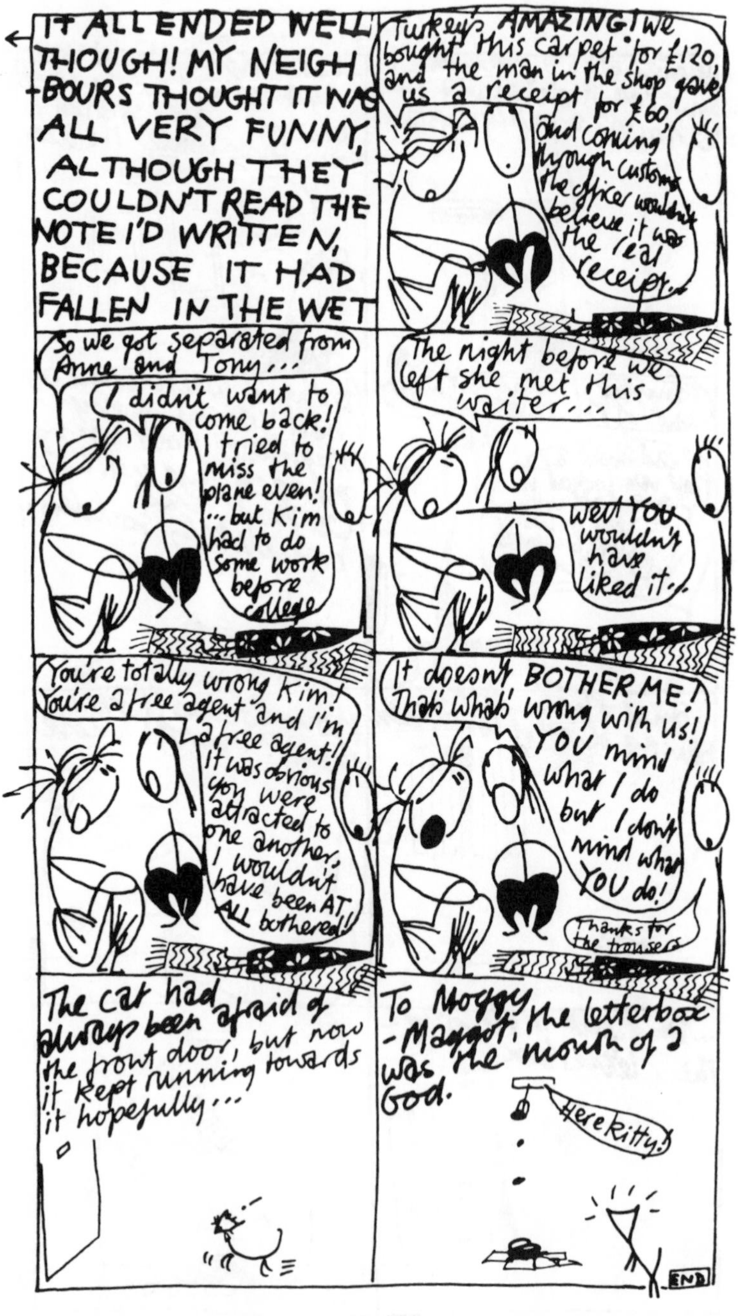
IT ALL ENDED WELL THOUGH! MY NEIGH-BOURS THOUGHT IT WAS ALL VERY FUNNY, ALTHOUGH THEY COULDN'T READ THE NOTE I'D WRITTEN, BECAUSE IT HAD FALLEN IN THE WET
Turkey's AMAZING! We bought this carpet for £120, and the man in the shop gave us a receipt for £60, and coming through customs the officer wouldn't believe it was the real receipt...
So we got separated from Anne and Tony...
I didn't want to come back! I tried to miss the plane even! ...but Kim had to do some work before college
The night before we left she met this waiter...
Well YOU wouldn't have liked it...
You're totally wrong Kim! You're a free agent and I'm a free agent! It was obvious you were attracted to one another, I wouldn't have been AT ALL bothered!
It doesn't BOTHER ME! That's what's wrong with us! YOU mind what I do but I don't mind what YOU do!
Thanks for the trousers
The cat had always been afraid of the front door, but now it kept running towards it hopefully...
To Moggy-Maggot, the letterbox was the mouth of a God.
Here Kitty!
END

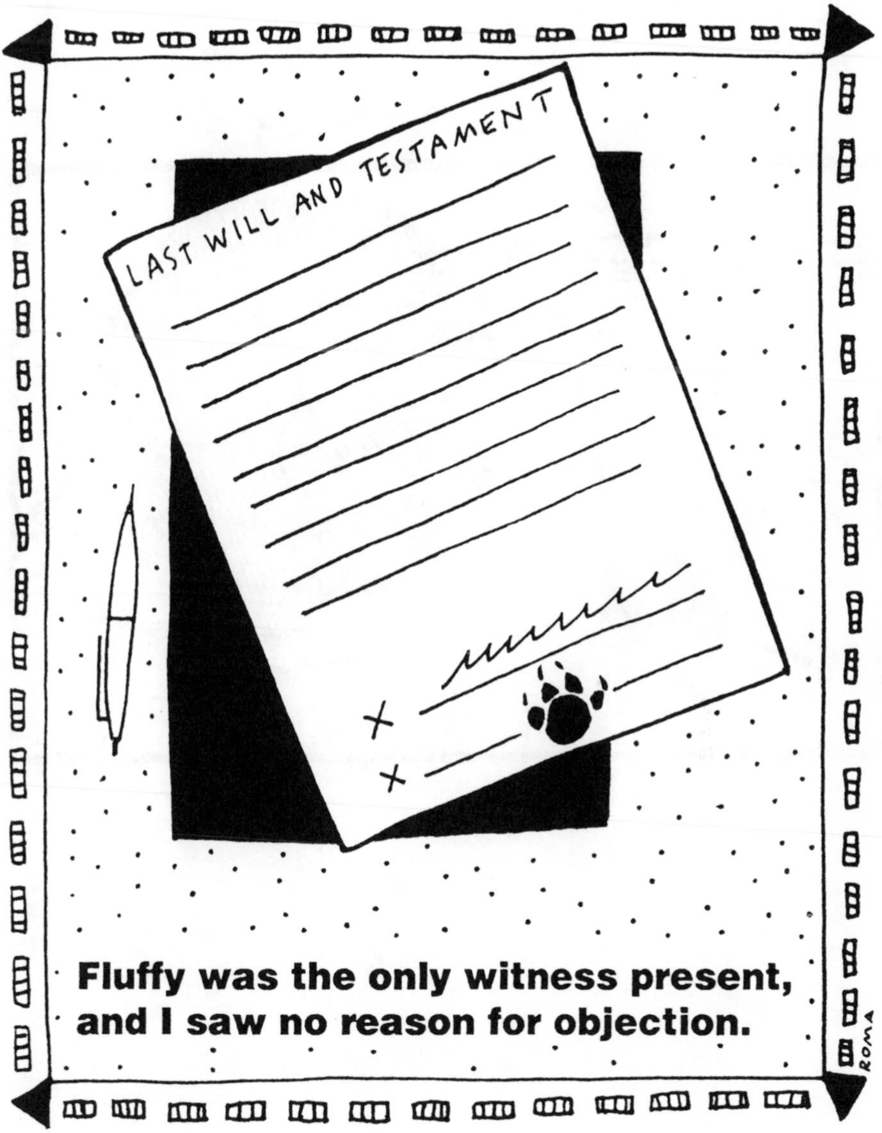
LAST WILL AND TESTAMENT
ROMA

Fluffy was the only witness present, and I saw no reason for objection.

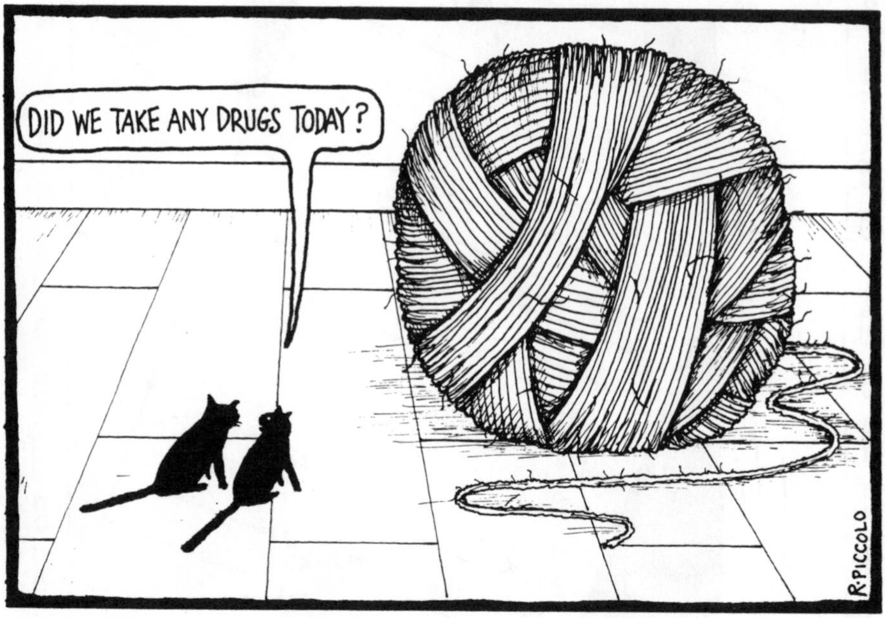
DID WE TAKE ANY DRUGS TODAY?
R·PICCOLO

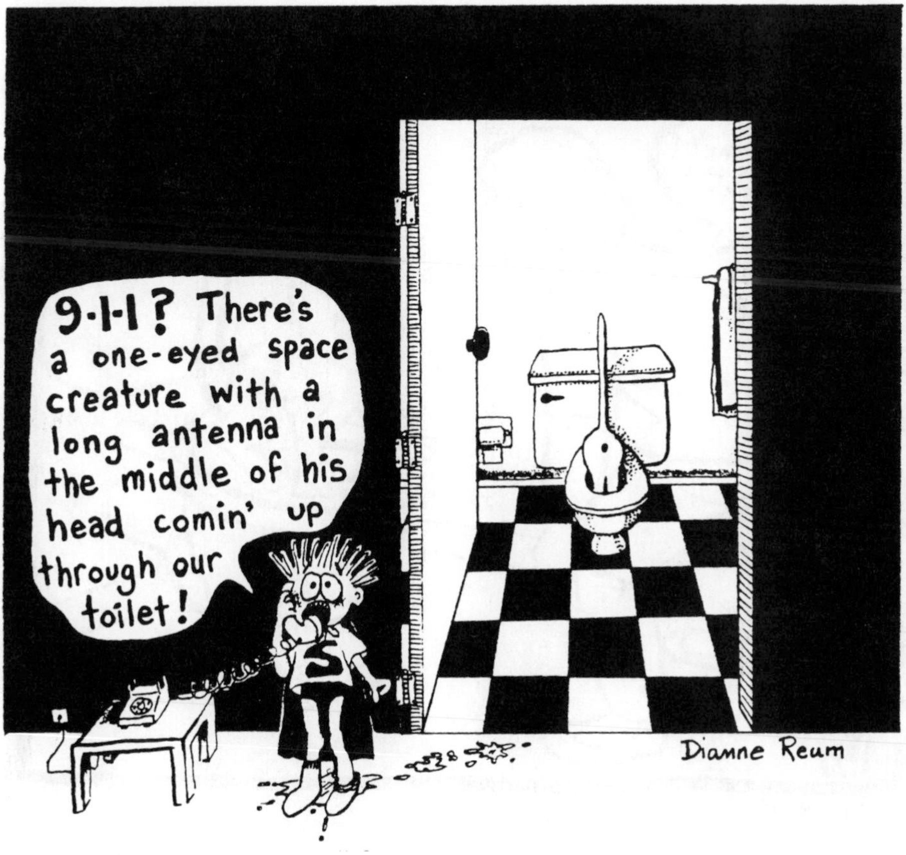
9·1·1? There's a one-eyed space creature with a long antenna in the middle of his head comin' up through our toilet!
Dianne Reum

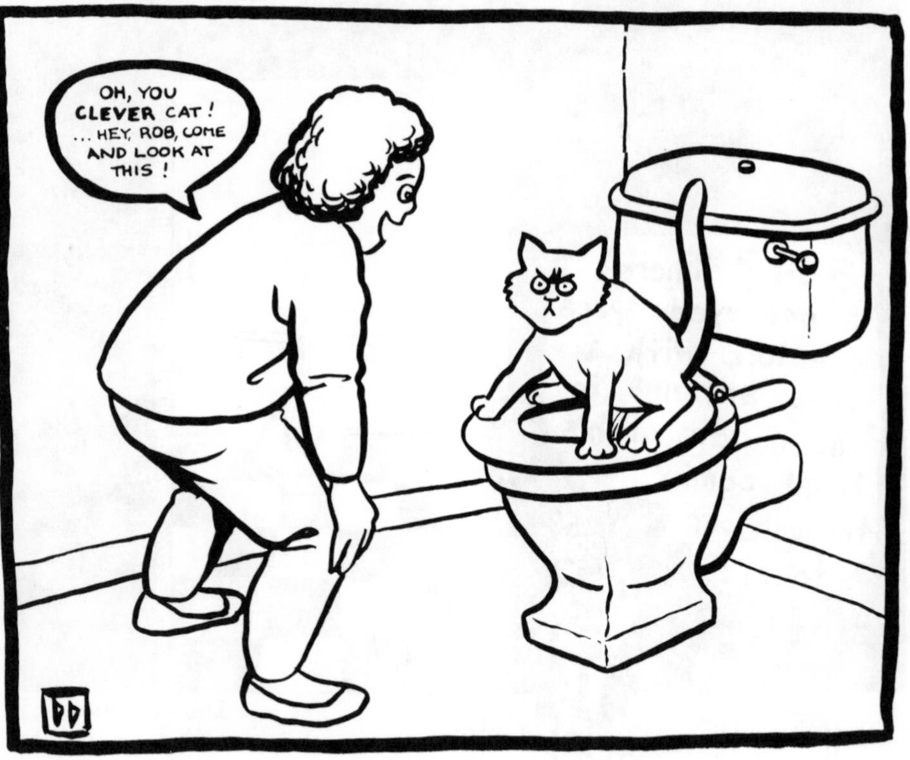
OH, YOU CLEVER CAT! ... HEY, ROB, COME AND LOOK AT THIS!

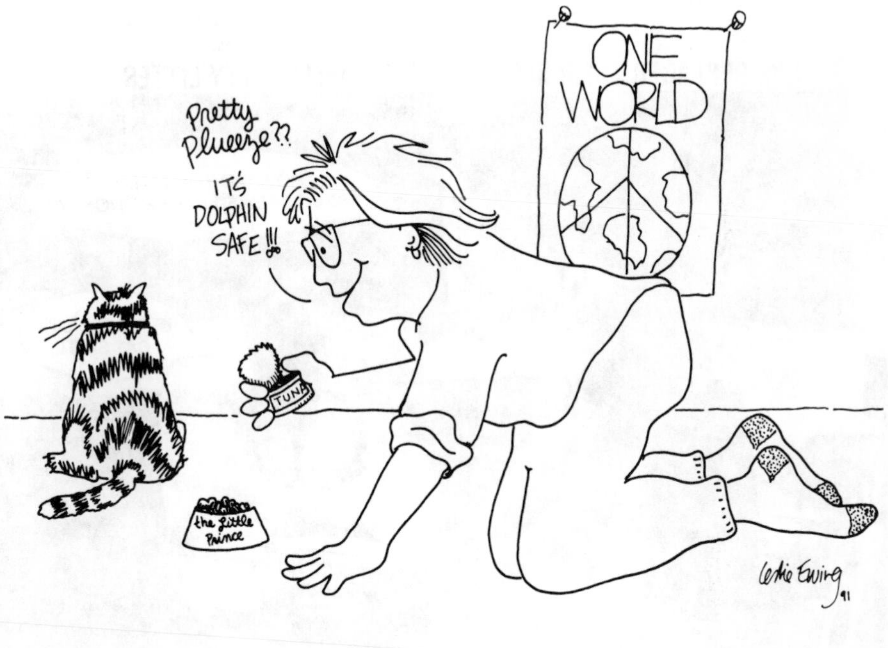
ONE
WORLD
Pretty
Pluueeze??
IT'S
DOLPHIN
SAFE!!!
TUNA
the Little
Prince
Leslie Ewing '91

SHE REPLACED THEIR REGULAR COFFEE WITH KITTY LITTER . . .

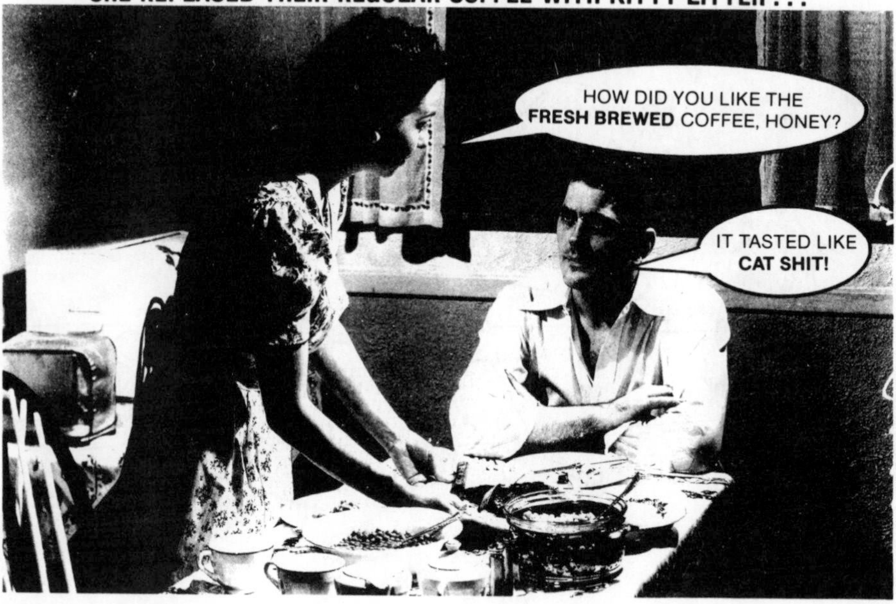
HOW DID YOU LIKE THE **FRESH BREWED** COFFEE, HONEY?
IT TASTED LIKE **CAT SHIT!**

Mary Lawton

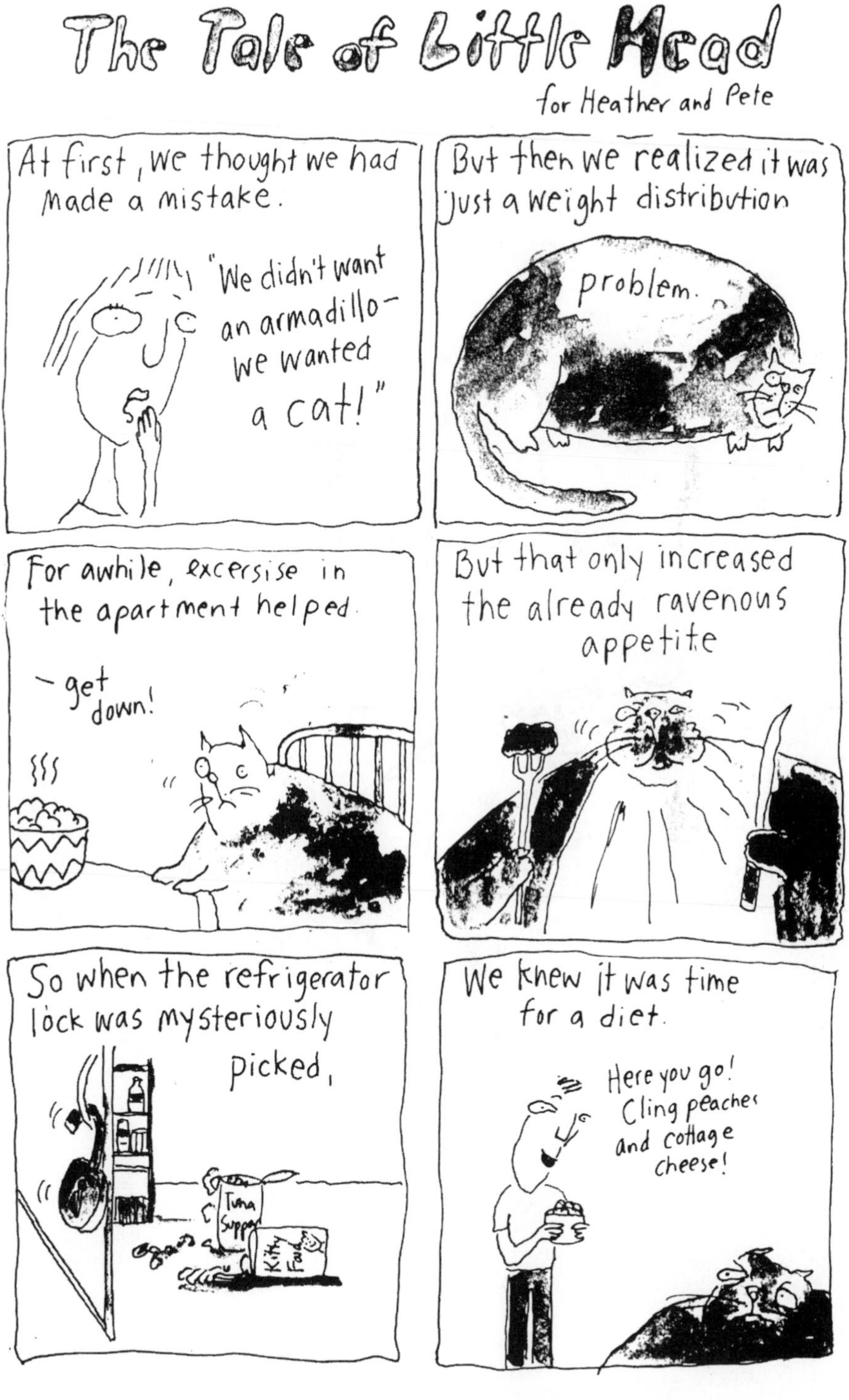
The Tale of Little Head
for Heather and Pete
At first, we thought we had made a mistake.
"We didn't want an armadillo- we wanted a cat!"
But then we realized it was just a weight distribution
problem.
For awhile, excersise in the apartment helped.
- get down!
But that only increased the already ravenous appetite
So when the refrigerator lock was mysteriously picked,
Tuna Supper
Kitty Food
We knew it was time for a diet.
Here you go! Cling peaches and cottage cheese!

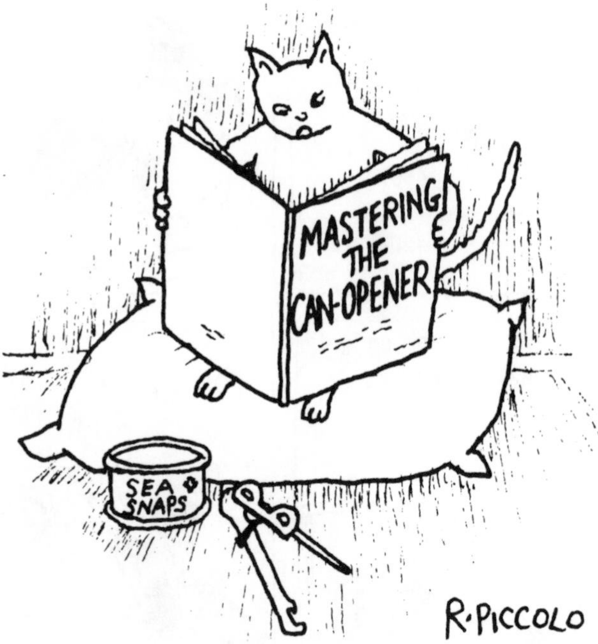
MASTERING THE CAN-OPENER
SEA SNAPS
R·PICCOLO

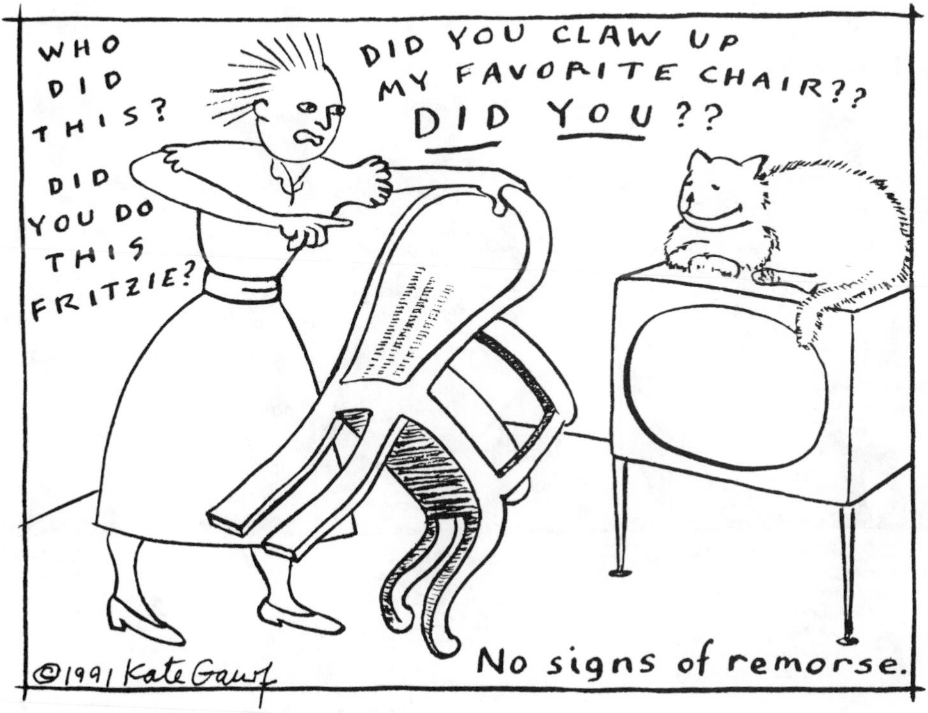
WHO DID THIS?
DID YOU DO THIS FRITZIE?
DID YOU CLAW UP MY FAVORITE CHAIR?? DID YOU??
No signs of remorse.
©1991 Kate Gawf

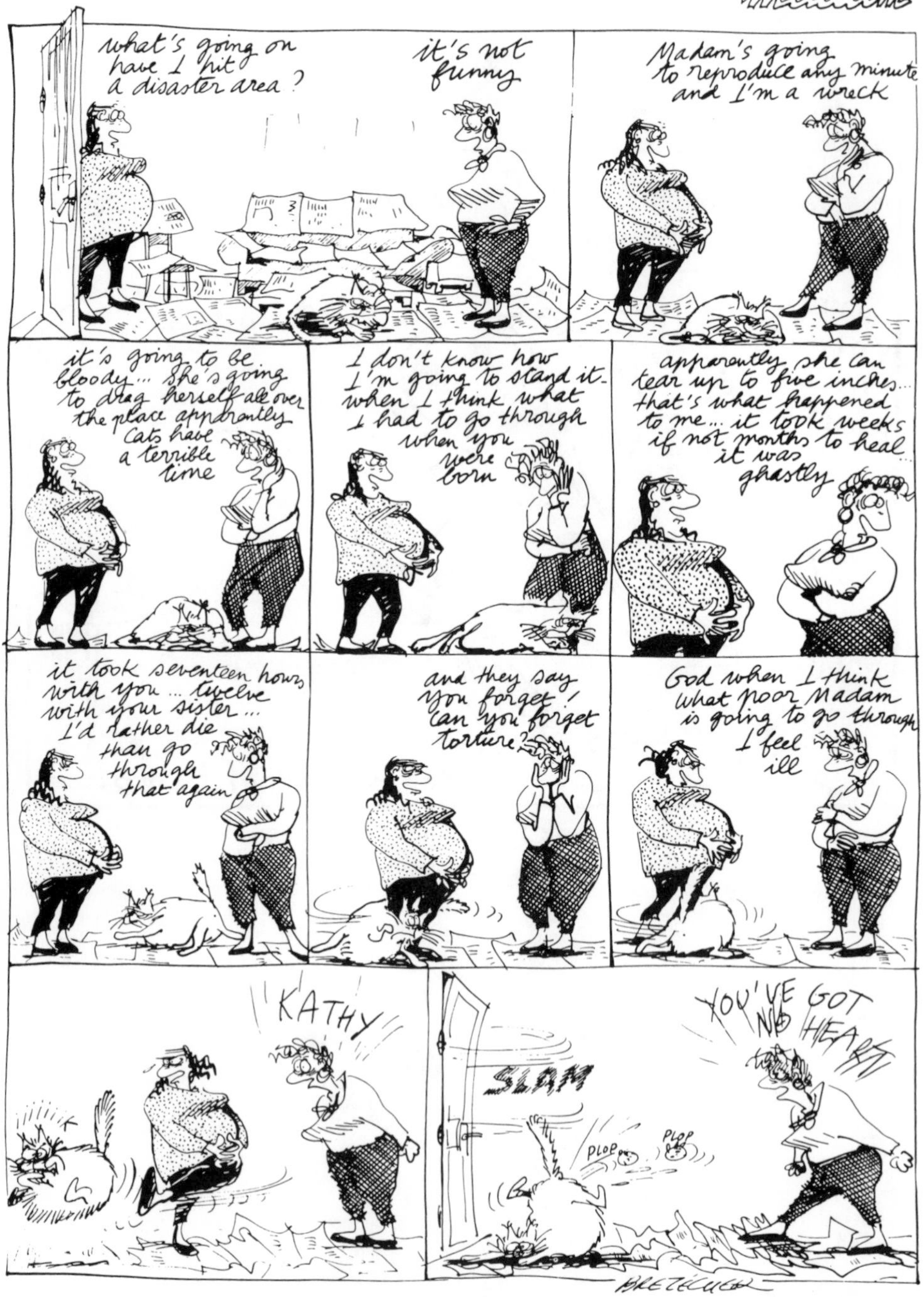
madam
what's going on have I hit a disaster area?
it's not funny
Madam's going to reproduce any minute and I'm a wreck
it's going to be bloody... she's going to drag herself all over the place apparently cats have a terrible time
I don't know how I'm going to stand it when I think what I had to go through when you were born
apparently she can tear up to five inches... that's what happened to me... it took weeks if not months to heal... it was ghastly
it took seventeen hours with you... twelve with your sister... I'd rather die than go through that again
and they say you forget! can you forget torture?
God when I think what poor Madam is going to go through I feel ill
KATHY
YOU'VE GOT NO HEART
SLAM
PLOP
PLOP
BRETECHER

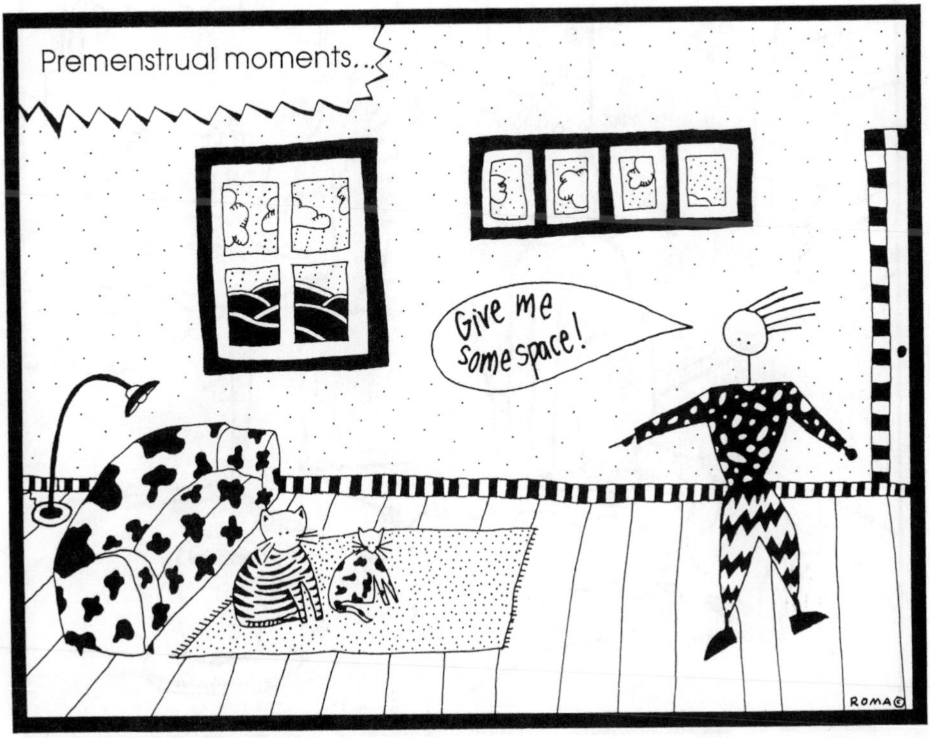
Premenstrual moments...
Give me some space!
ROMA©

"I have to close now— Mr. Muffins feels we need to process."

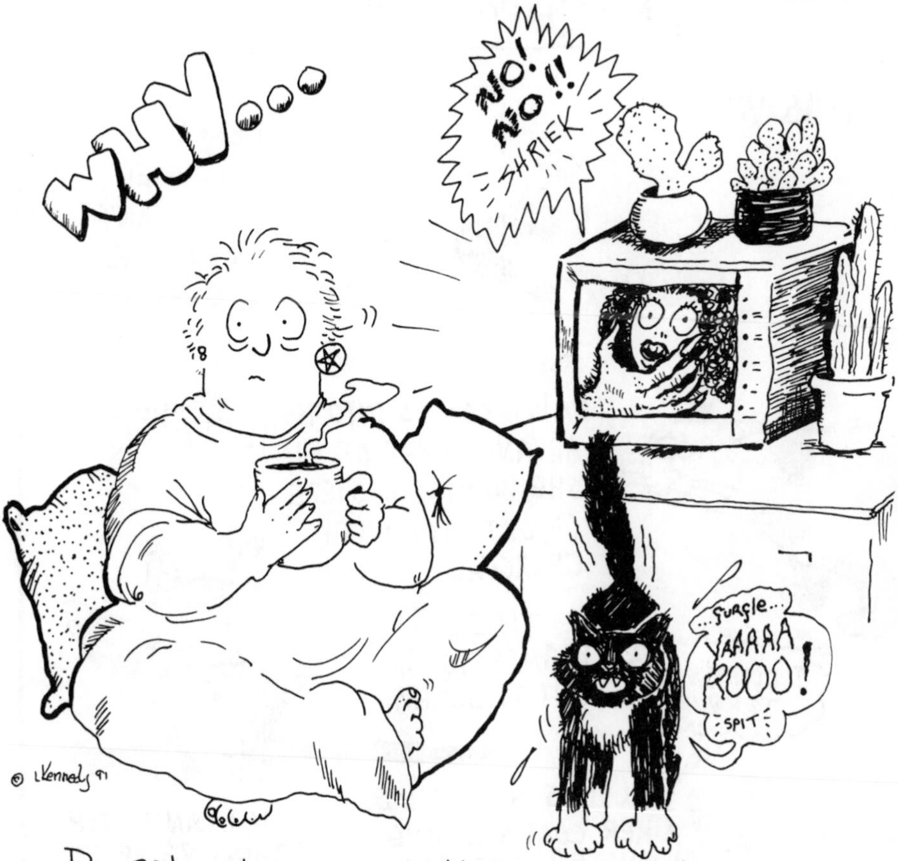
WHY...
NO! NO!! SHRIEK
...gurgle...
YAARRA ROOO!
SPIT
© L Kennedy 91

Do cats always see things you can't see when you're on your own, it's late, and there's something scary on TV?

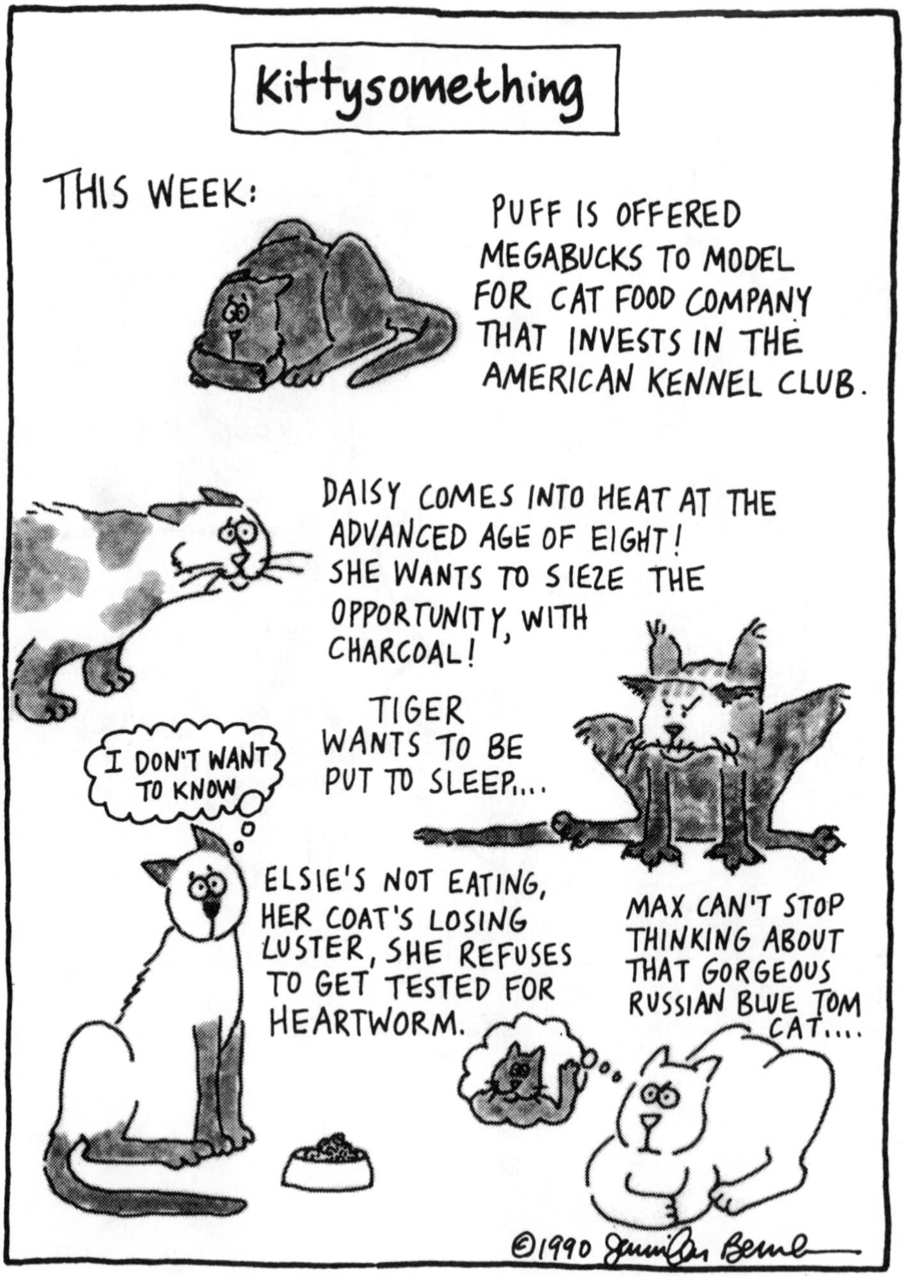
Kittysomething
THIS WEEK:
PUFF IS OFFERED MEGABUCKS TO MODEL FOR CAT FOOD COMPANY THAT INVESTS IN THE AMERICAN KENNEL CLUB.
DAISY COMES INTO HEAT AT THE ADVANCED AGE OF EIGHT! SHE WANTS TO SIEZE THE OPPORTUNITY, WITH CHARCOAL!
TIGER WANTS TO BE PUT TO SLEEP....
I DON'T WANT TO KNOW
ELSIE'S NOT EATING, HER COAT'S LOSING LUSTER, SHE REFUSES TO GET TESTED FOR HEARTWORM.
MAX CAN'T STOP THINKING ABOUT THAT GORGEOUS RUSSIAN BLUE TOM CAT....
©1990 Jennifer Berman

"TIME FOR MY FAVORITE SOAP OPERA: 'NINE LIVES TO LIVE.' "

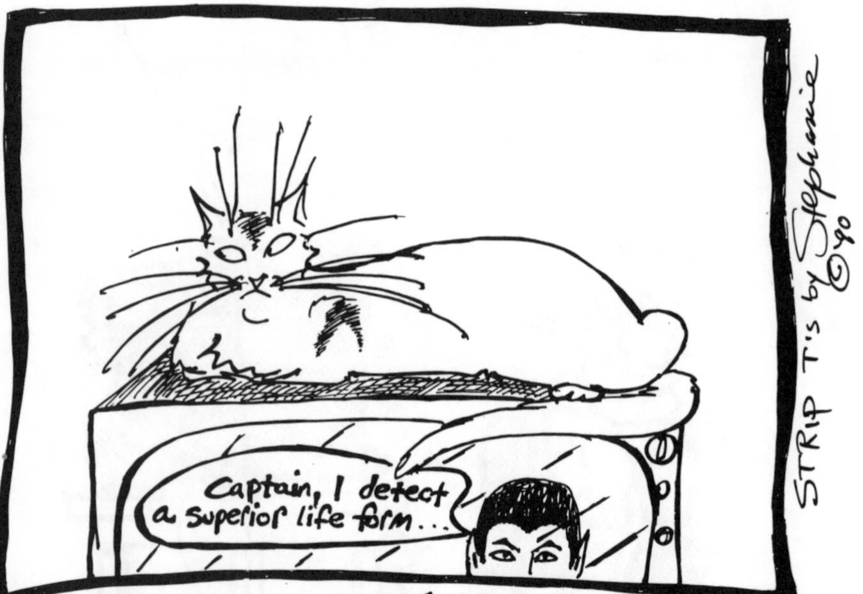
Captain, I detect a superior life form...
STRIP T's by Stephanie ©'90

She found him in the parking lot of the Trekkie convention... she decided he was Part Siamese... and Part Vulcan...

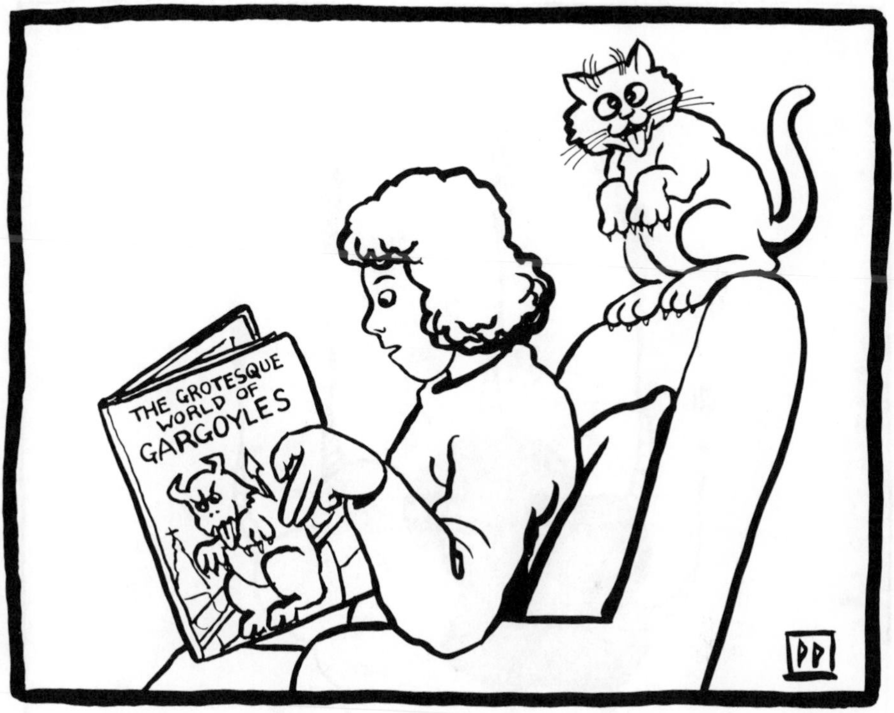
THE GROTESQUE WORLD OF GARGOYLES
DD

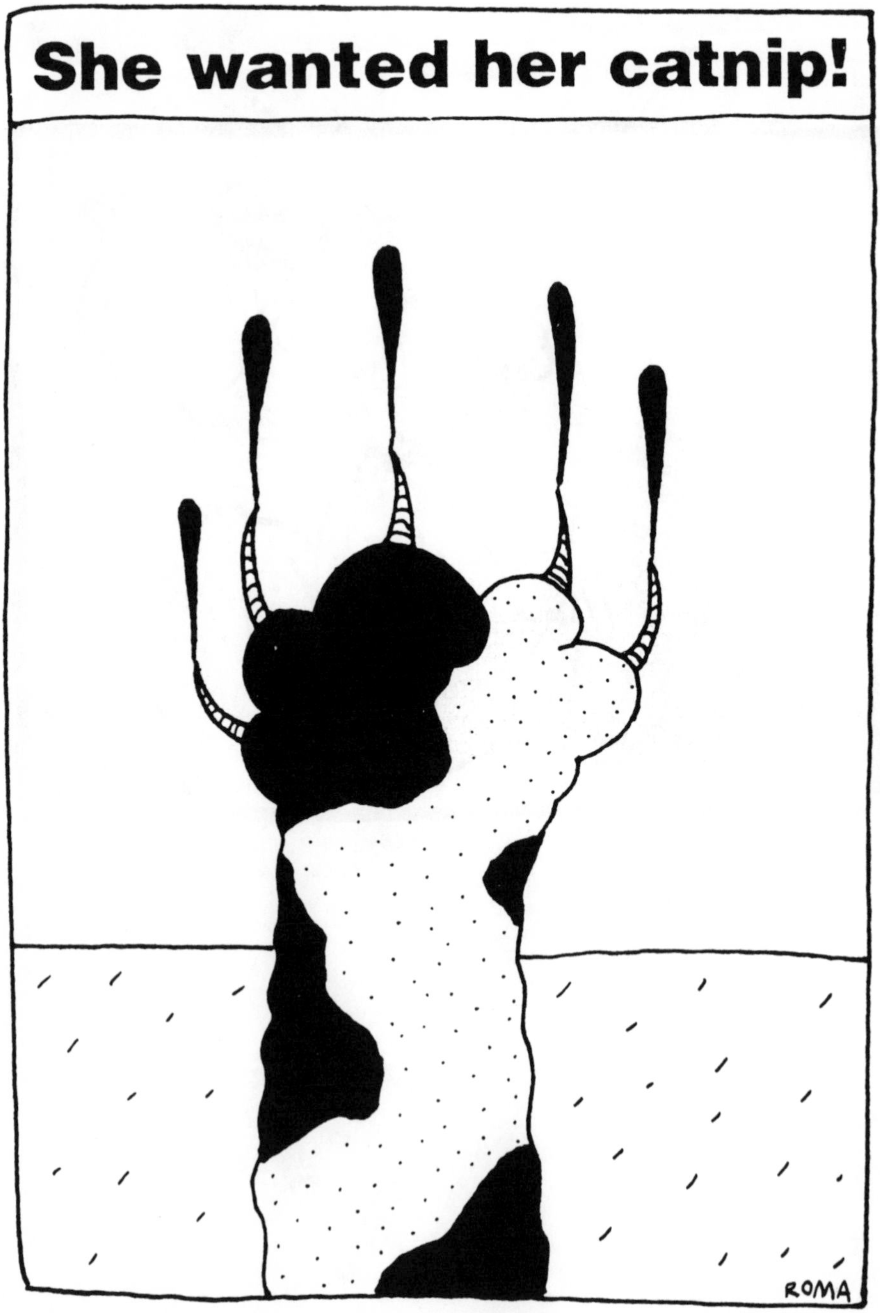
She wanted her catnip!
ROMA

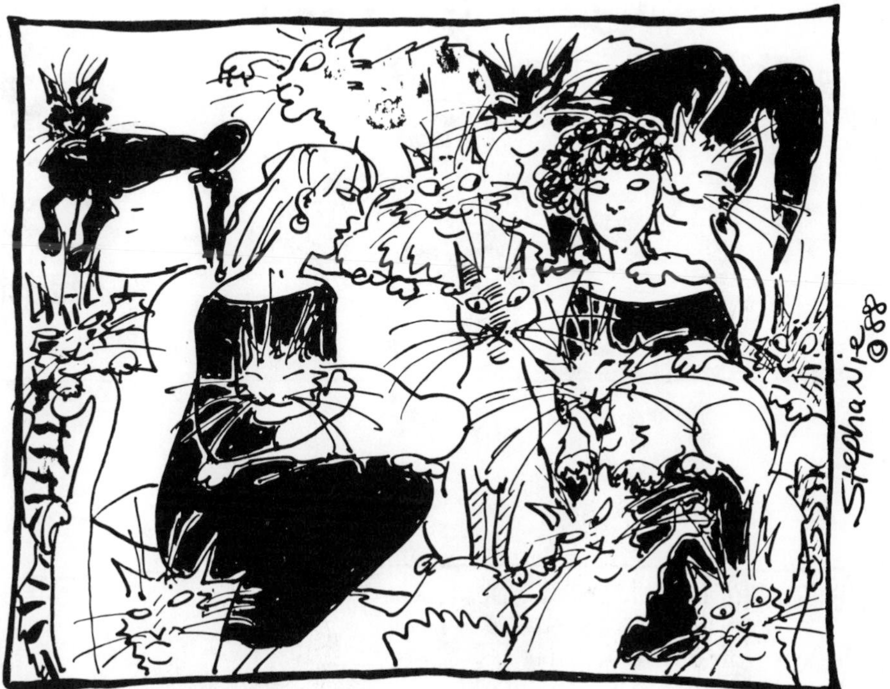
Stephanie ©88

"It's taken me years... but I now have one in every color!"

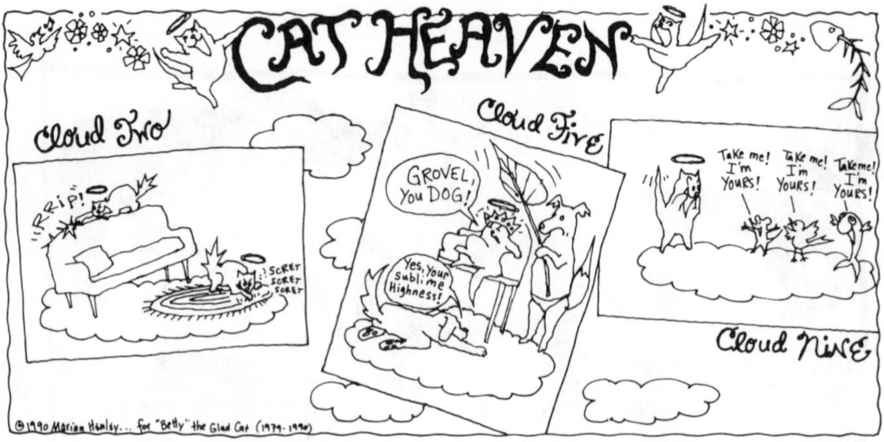
CAT HEAVEN
Cloud Two
RRIP!
SCRET SCRET SCRET
Cloud Five
GROVEL, YOU DOG!
Yes, Your Sublime Highness!
Take me! I'm YOURS!
Take me! I'm YOURS!
Take me! I'm YOURS!
Cloud Nine
©1990 Marian Henley... for "Betty" the Glad Cat (1979-1990)

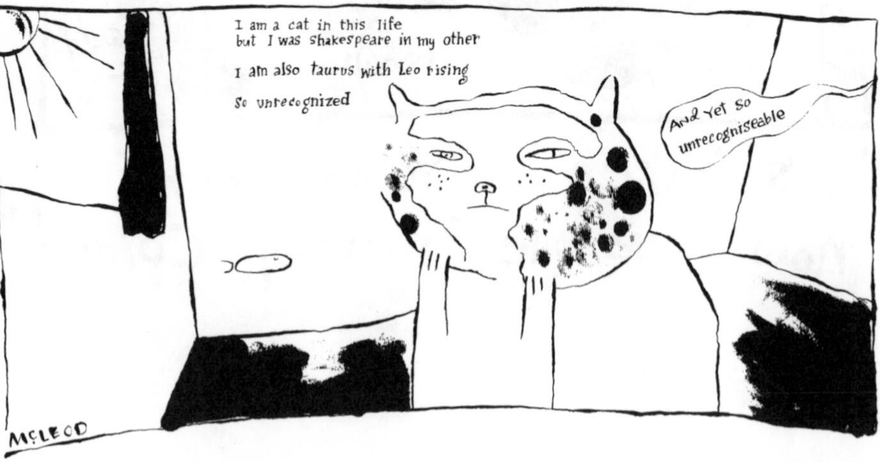
I am a cat in this life
but I was shakespeare in my other
I am also taurus with Leo rising
so unrecognized
And yet so unrecognizeable
McLEOD

Mette Thomsen/Chris Suddick

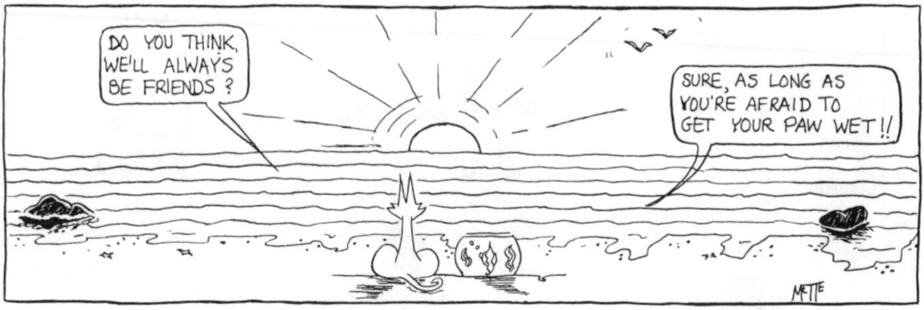
DO YOU THINK, WE'LL ALWAYS BE FRIENDS ?
SURE, AS LONG AS YOU'RE AFRAID TO GET YOUR PAW WET !!
METTE

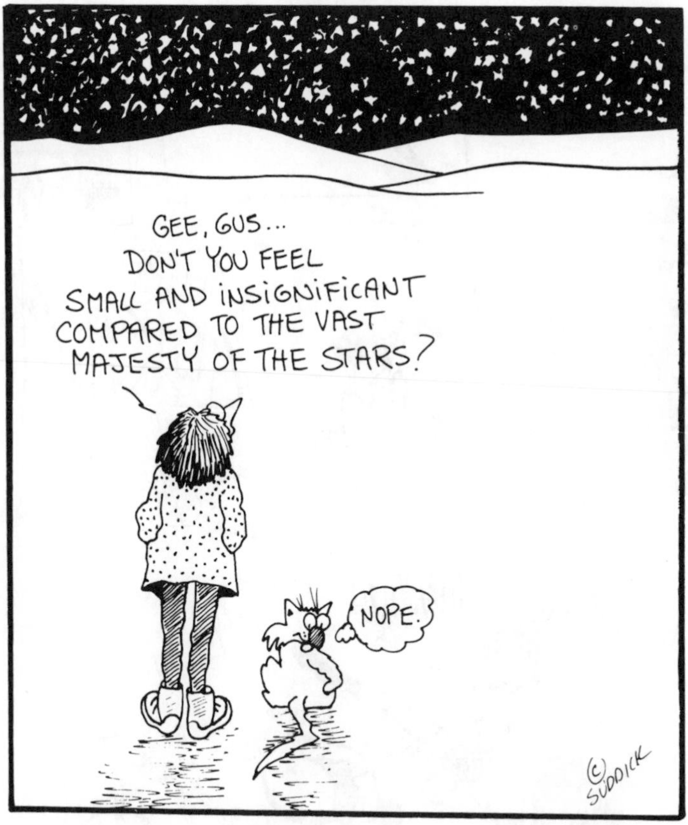
GEE, GUS... DON'T YOU FEEL SMALL AND INSIGNIFICANT COMPARED TO THE VAST MAJESTY OF THE STARS?
NOPE.
© SUDDICK

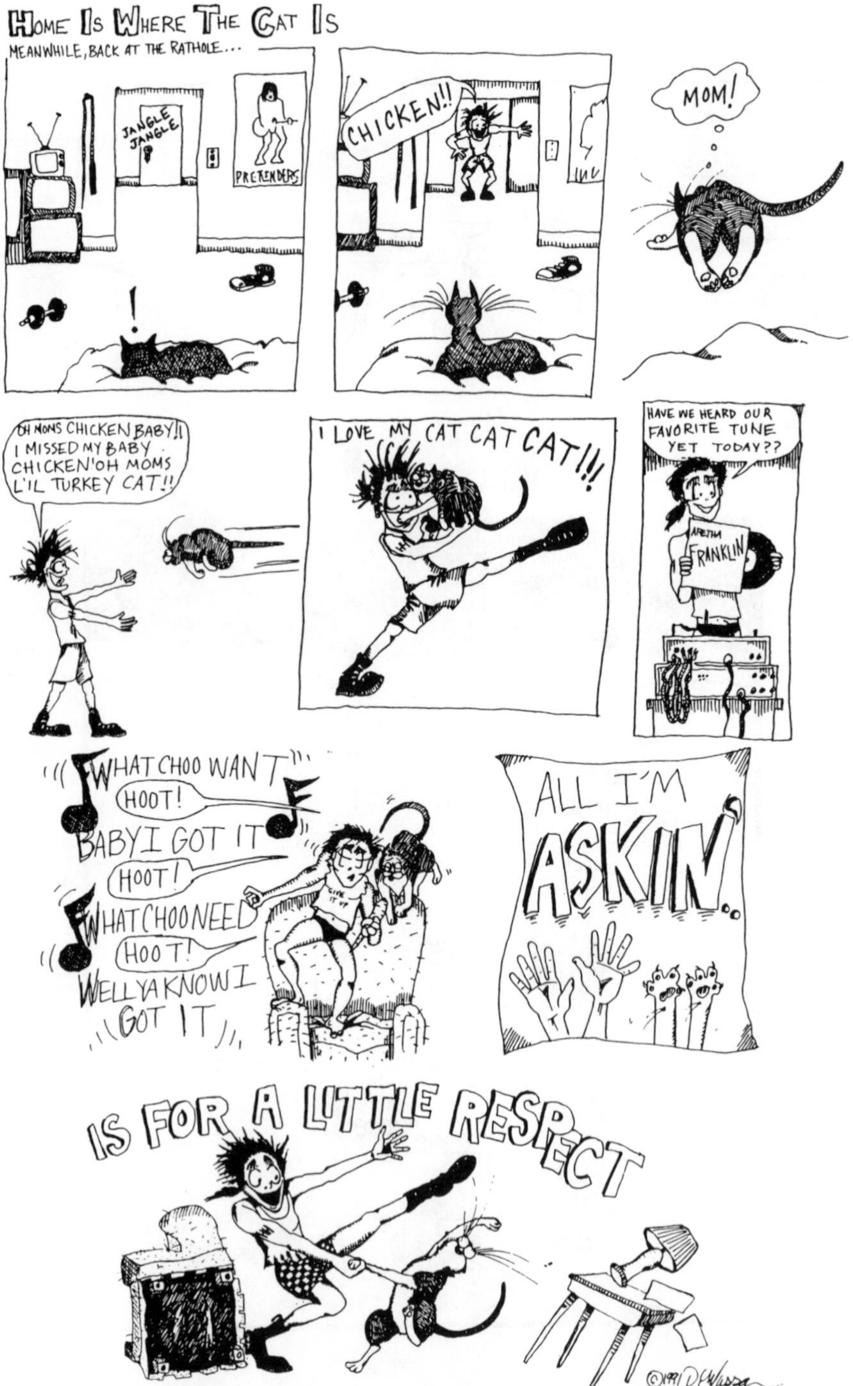
HOME IS WHERE THE CAT IS
MEANWHILE, BACK AT THE RATHOLE...
JANGLE JANGLE
PRETENDERS
!
CHICKEN!!
MOM!
OH MOMS CHICKEN BABY!! I MISSED MY BABY CHICKEN! OH MOMS L'IL TURKEY CAT!!
I LOVE MY CAT CAT CAT CAT!!!
HAVE WE HEARD OUR FAVORITE TUNE YET TODAY??
ARETHA FRANKLIN
WHAT CHOO WANT
HOOT!
BABY I GOT IT
HOOT!
WHAT CHOO NEED
HOOT!
WELL YA KNOW I GOT IT
ALL I'M ASKIN'..
IS FOR A LITTLE RESPECT

If you enjoyed *Kitty Libber* you may enjoy Roz Warren's other books:

> ***Women's Glib, A Collection of Women's Humor:*** Cartoons,
> stories and poems by America's funniest women wits that
> will knock you off your chair laughing. $10.95
> ***Women's Glibber:*** Madonna! Sex! Poultry! and much
> more. State-of-the-art feminist humor on a wide range of
> topics. Available September 1992. $10.95
> ***Women's Glib, Cartoon Engagement Calendar 1993:*** Hilari-
> ous quotes, cartoons and light verse by leading women
> humorists for every week of the year. $ 9.95

These books are available at your local bookstore or you can order directly from us.
Use the coupon below, or call toll-free at 800-777-1048. Please have your VISA or
Mastercard ready.

Humor Books by Rosalind Warren

Please send me _____ copies of *Kitty Libber* at $ 8.95
_____ copies of *Women's Glib* at $ 10.95
_____ copies of *Women's Glibber* at $ 10.95
_____ copies of *Women's Glib, A Cartoon Engagement Calendar 1993* at $9.95

Postage & handling: Please include $ 2.00 for first book and an additional .50 for each book thereafter for book rate delivery.

Total Enclosed _____ Check #_____

VISA or Mastercard # _____ Expires _____

Name _____

Address _____

Mail payment to: The Crossing Press, P.O. Box 1048, Freedom CA 95019